2000 Y
OF SMALL
GROUPS

2000 YEARS OF SMALL GROUPS

A HISTORY OF CELL MINISTRY IN THE CHURCH

JOEL COMISKEY, PH.D.

CCS Publishing
www.joelcomiskeygroup.com

Published by CCS Publishing
23890 Brittlebush Circle
Moreno Valley, CA 92557 USA
1-888-511-9995

Printed in the United States of America.

Cover design: Jason Klanderud
Editor: Scott Boren

ISBN: 978-1-935789-59-8
LCCN: 2014901957

CCS Publishing is the book-publishing division of Joel Comiskey Group, a resource and coaching ministry dedicated to equipping leaders for cell-based ministry.
Find us on the World Wide Web at www.joelcomiskeygroup.com

PRAISES FOR
2000 Years of Small Groups

"God has blessed the modern Home Cell Movement with the heart, vision, and writing skills of Joel Comiskey! This book will become a classic, a documentary that has recorded the movement up to this present generation. One of its greatest contributions is to guide those who will participate in the further growth of the movement."
—Dr. Ralph W. Neighbour, Jr., author, professor, and church planter

Joel Comiskey has given us a gift—a historical and global view of the small group movement. He describes how group life is not a fad rather, it's been an essential expression of church life for 2,000 years without which we cannot make Christ-centered disciples.
—Dr. Bill Donahue, Professor and best-selling author of Leading Life-changing Small Groups

"This is the most thoroughly researched, carefully documented and clearly written book on this topic I have ever seen. Dr. Comiskey rightly demonstrates that small-group and cell-based Christian fellowships have been and are timelessly central, essential, and integral aspects of the life of the Church. In this day of our enthusiasm over large and spectacular mega-churches, we need to heed Comiskey's prophetic and wise word. This is must reading for anyone interested or involved in cell-based or small-group ministry anywhere in the world."
—Dr. Chuck Van Engen, *Arthur F. Glasser Professor of Biblical Theology at Fuller Theological Seminary, School of Intercultural Studies*

"In this timely book, Joel Comiskey shows conclusively that small groups are essential, not a recent innovation. Wherever the church has been vital and growing and serious about discipleship, small groups have abounded. Comiskey's historical overview, punctuated by brief "Lessons Learned" summaries, is a valuable addition to current discussions about the church and discipleship. By going back well before the Protestant Reformation, Comiskey clarifies the key link between church vitality and face-to-face community all through history. Yet Comiskey wisely warns of the danger of taking any one small-group or cell-church model as the perfect solution for every time and place. Principles endure; applications vary. I am happy to recommend this book to Christians who want to see the church thrive faithfully in our day."
—Howard Snyder, *Author; formerly professor at Asbury Theological Seminary (Kentucky, USA) and Tyndale Seminary (Toronto, Canada)*

TABLE OF CONTENTS

ACKNOWLEDGEMENTS

This book is so much better because of the many people who contributed to it.

Scott Boren, my primary editor, did another thorough job of editing this book and offering rock solid advice about its formation. Scott sees the book in the early stages and gives me valuable insight on big picture ideas and themes.

Anne White thoroughly copy-edited the book during the final stages before publication. .God has given her an eye for detail, and I depend on her expertise. She offered advice on critical grammatical questions and improved this book greatly. I first met Anne during my Ph.D. days at Fuller Seminary, where she was editing doctoral degrees for students like myself. I'm grateful for her friendship and help in perfecting this book.

I want to thank Patricia Barrett for her copy-editing help in this book. She loves history and spent a lot of time making this book better.

Bill Joukhadar has volunteered his copy-editing skills on most of my books and did the same for this one. He found errors that were overlooked by others, and I greatly appreciate his friendship and hard work.

Rae Holt has been a long-term supporter of Joel Comiskey Group, and I'm very thankful that he once again took the time to offer his critique and suggestions for this book.

Jay Stanwood did a very thorough job of looking at this book and making key suggestions. He always does a great job of helping me to formulate my sentences in a more precise way. I appreciate the way he suggests new phrases and sentence structure.

I also want to thank my good friend Jim Egli for allowing me to use portions of his excellent paper on the history of the cell church for the last chapter of this book.

INTRODUCTION

In a growing church in South Korea, a pastor collapsed while preaching God's Word. The physical exhaustion of his ministry was too much for him to bear. His doctors told him he would have to stop preaching and would be confined to his bed. So he laid in bed and while reading the Bible, looked for ministry alternatives. He rediscovered accounts of the ancient New Testament house churches in the book of Acts as well as the organizational structure given to Moses from his father-in-law, Jethro, in Exodus chapter eighteen. From this revelation came the founding of what is now called the cell church or the cell-based church. David Cho's crisis of faith and the resulting transformation of his church has resulted in a worldwide movement of churches that put small groups at the center of life and ministry. Although this model of church life began in an Assemblies of God Church in Korea, it has been embraced by churches of many denominations and in many nations. Its impact has been so far-reaching that today many of the largest churches in the world are cell-based.

Of course this new movement wasn't really new at all. There were simply progressive waves of the movement appearing and disappearing over time. It started with the early church, moved through Monasticism, and continued in an ever increasing vibrancy to the modern day cell movement. Some speculate that the cell movement that began at the end of the twentieth century is the beginning of a second reformation that will ultimately transform the church on a scale similar to the reformation that began in the sixteenth century.[1]

But is a second reformation too optimistic and even speculative? The reason people believe it to be a second reformation is because the priesthood of all believers was never fully realized in the first reformation. The church forms and building structures that were deeply embedded in Europe and later in North America hindered the full implementation of the priesthood of all believers.

Some of the movements that tried to reform the state church, like the Waldensians, Lollards, Hussites, Anabaptists, and Pietists, emphasized homes as meeting places for believers, but the state church continued to be the norm for most believers. Yet beginning with the Moravians, John Wesley, the house church movement, and now the modern day cell church movement, small group ministry has become the new norm in many places around the world.

The reality is that God has used small group ministry throughout church history to disciple, revive, consolidate, and evangelize.

---

1. This speculation has been put forward by Carl George in his book, *Prepare Your Church for the Future,* and author Ralph Neighbour, Jr. in his book, *Where Do We Go From Here?* Bill Beckham's book, *The Second Reformation* brings those arguments together in one book.

Although small groups played an important role in the Old Testament (Exodus 18), Jesus took small group ministry to a new level by creating his own band of followers and then sending them to start house churches. We know that the early church was a movement of networked house churches that spread over the world and triumphed over the sword. Historian Herbert Butterfield captures the historical importance of the small group,

> The strongest organizational unit in the world's history would appear to be that which we call a cell because it is a remorseless self-multiplier; is exceptionally difficult to destroy; can preserve its intensity of local life while vast organizations quickly wither when they are weakened at the center; can defy the power of governments; is the appropriate lever for prying open any status quo . . . this seems the appointed way by which a mere handful of people may open up a new chapter in the history of civilization.[2]

Small groups throughout Church history have helped purify the church and return it to its historic roots. Some movements imitated the primitive New Testament church very closely while others could only take baby steps because of external political pressure or debilitating church traditions. As I researched these historical eras and the leaders associated with them, I gained new compassion for small groups and a certain bonding with their ideas, persistence, and love for the Church of Jesus Christ. I hope you will too.

---

2. As quoted in William A. Beckham, *The Two Winged Church Will Fly* (Houston, TX: Touch Publications, 1993), p. 119.

Chapter 1

SMALL GROUPS IN BIBLICAL PERSPETIVE

Picture yourself traveling down a Roman road on your way to attend a first century house church. As you walk down the narrow streets, you notice people everywhere. You're well aware of the over-population of Rome—where approximately one million people live—with the vast majority crowded in one or two room apartments above or behind shops and markets. You admire some of the larger homes as you make your way down the narrow road, but you also notice that most of the dwelling places are small single rooms.

You finally arrive at the home, which is really an apartment. It's a residential unit with an adjoining courtyard and you notice several rows of apartments connected to each other. You remember from your previous trips to this house that the neighbors are very quizzical about the gathering because they can hear the singing and even some of the conversations. You once again reflect on the crowded conditions of Rome due to the constant influx of immigrants. Privacy is almost impossible here.

As you enter the home, the rich smell of food fills the air. You notice the food baking outside while you are ushered into the dining area, the largest room in the house. Like most apartments in the area, this one is made of timber and mud brick, making it prone to fire and collapse. The apartment also has an upper floor but like most places, there is no central heating, running water, or lavatory.

You count thirteen people at the gathering and all have been invited to share the meal together—in memory of Jesus Christ. The story of Christ's last supper with his disciples in the upper room makes Christ's presence seem so real to you. You love the testimonies of changed lives, and people's love for this risen Jesus. You hear stories about those who actually saw Jesus after his resurrection. And they say that Jesus promised to return quickly. Other stories of Christ's miracles are repeated. You love the natural free-flowing atmosphere, the singing, the Scripture reading, and the expectation of the Holy Spirit's presence.

Your experience in the house church that night is emotional and vibrant. You feel God's joy as you talk with like-minded believers and remember that Jesus is also present in spirit. As you reflect on being born again one year earlier during your first meeting, you are grateful to be Christ's follower and a participant in such a loving group of believers. Your supreme desire is to spread the good news of the gospel to everyone you meet. After all, Jesus is coming soon.

JESUS AND HOUSE-TO-HOUSE MINISTRY

The above story illustrates how the early church met, and it reflects much of the way that Jesus ministered. He could have built a lavish synagogue or even renovated the existing temple in Jerusalem, but he didn't. On the other hand, some see Jesus sleeping in tents around campfires with his disciples, conjuring up images of cowboys in the wild, wild West.

The truth is that Jesus primarily ministered in a household setting. When reading about Jesus going from village to village and healing the sick, he was actually ministering in homes. The following offers a glimpse of Christ's home ministry:

- Jesus in the house of Peter (Matthew 8:14)
- Jesus in the house of Matthew (Matthew 9:10)
- Jesus in the house of Zacchaeus (Luke 19:1-10)
- Jesus in the house of Lazarus and his sisters (Luke 10:38-42)
- Jesus in the house of Jairus (Mark 5:35-38)
- Jesus healing two blind people in a house (Matthew 9:28-30)
- Jesus in the house of Simon the Leper (Matthew 26:6)
- Jesus teaching his disciples in a house (Mark 7:17-18; 9:33, 10:10)
- Jesus forgiving and healing a paralyzed person in a house (Luke 5:19)

- Jesus in the home of a pharisee (Luke 14:1)
- Jesus instituting the Lord's Supper in a house (Matthew 26:18)
- Jesus sending his twelve and his seventy disciples to heal and teach from village to village and house-to-house (Luke 9:1-9; 10:1-11)

Jesus also had a house church base, which was the home of Peter. In Luke 4:38-40 we read,

> Jesus left the synagogue and went to the home of Simon. Now Simon's mother-in-law was suffering from a high fever, and they asked Jesus to help her. So he bent over her and rebuked the fever, and it left her. She got up at once and began to wait on them. When the sun was setting, the people brought to Jesus all who had various kinds of sickness, and laying his hands on each one, he healed them.

Not only did Peter and Andrew live there, but a network of evangelistic contacts grew from that home, including friends of the family. Most likely Peter's house was a place where Jesus and his disciples could pray, enjoy community, and develop spiritually. It also served as a meeting room and place of healing and instruction. You might even call it the first model house church.[1]

In addition to the house of Peter in Capernaum, we read of Zacchaeus in Jericho, the head of a household who became a follower of Jesus (Luke 19:1-10). It's also likely that Jesus won some of his early disciples through house-to-house ministry

1. Roger W. Gehring, *House Church and Mission: The Importance of Household Structures in Early Christianity* (Peabody, MA: Hendrickson, 2004), p. 47.

(Luke 10:5-6) who lived in Galilee (Mark 1:29-31), Judea (Matthew 24:16), and in the Decapolis region (Mark 5:19-20).

One key reason Jesus chose the home as his operational headquarters was because he wanted to create a new spiritual family. And to make this happen, he first had to transform people where they lived and where essential character values were displayed. Jesus wanted to infuse the normal family network with a new vision of love and sacrifice. To do this, he lived among his disciples in houses, showing them practically how to love and serve one another (John 13:1-17). Christ's teaching on true greatness (using children as an example) takes place in the context of a house setting (Mark 9:33-36). He wanted his disciples to see servanthood as the central leadership style and childlike dependence as the guiding light.[2]

Jesus didn't simply gather them once a week for a "discipleship class." He lived with them, shared financial resources, and taught them about kingdom values. He didn't only instruct his disciples about how to pray, but asked them to accompany him to prayer meetings, so they could see him praying. When the disciples finally asked him what he was doing, he seized upon the opportunity to teach them about prayer (Luke 11:1-4). The disciples learned while doing, but they were also guided to carefully reflect on what they did.

When Jesus sent the disciples to do outreach, he chose the small home environment to proclaim his kingdom message. His goal was to reach an entire town and surrounding area. Luke 9 and 10 tell us that Jesus assigned the twelve and the

---

2. Carolyn Osiek, Margaret Y. MacDonald, Janet H. Tulloch, *A Women's Place: House Churches in Earliest Christianity* (Minneapolis, MI: Augsburg Fortress, 2006), Kindle edition, p. 83.

seventy-two disciples to go from village to village and to enter homes, offering peace to the inhabitants. Notice how Jesus sent them in pairs. He didn't want them to go alone. Each disciple needed a partner for fellowship, support, and ministry effectiveness. Jesus told them, "When you enter a house, first say, 'Peace to this house.' If a man of peace is there, your peace will rest on him; if not, it will return to you" (Luke 10:5-6). When they found a "man of peace" (one desiring to find peace), they remained in that home, eating and drinking whatever was set before them. Living in the home was a key part of Christ's ministry to reach the lost.

This peace message is actually the kingdom message, and all those who received Christ's kingdom proclamation were welcomed. Christ charged the disciples to heal the sick and preach the rule and authority of God, just as he did. As the disciples established the home base, or beachhead, they could then reach out and make more disciples.

The disciples were supposed to enter a home, convert the members of that particular household, and reach the other homes from a base location—rather than witnessing from house-to-house (Luke 10:7). Remaining in a house only makes sense if, beyond the initial proclamation of the kingdom message, the disciples stayed on to establish a faith community. The process then spread in ever widening circles, reaching its climax once the entire town had heard the kingdom message.

Christ sent his disciples without food and clothing telling them, "Do not take a purse or bag or sandals . . . Stay in that house, eating and drinking whatever they give you, for the worker deserves his wages" (Luke 10:4, 7). The disciples depended on the practical hospitality of the hosts, both for clothing and room and board. Roger Gehring, expert regarding early house churches, writes, "The radical charge to enter into mission without equipment and outfitting, to renounce all belongings, and thus to be dependent on the hospitality of houses surely corresponds with the attitude and practice of Jesus."[3]

Christ's house church strategy was the starting point for the ministry of the disciples after the resurrection. Christ's instructions as recorded in Luke 9 and 10 propelled the early church into house-to-house ministry. After Pentecost, as recorded in Acts 2, Christ's disciples followed his strategy by reaching the family household structure (*oikos*) with the gospel message and then reaching the entire city. One of the major reasons the early church was so effective was because they infiltrated the basic fabric of society—families living in homes. The reputed New Testament scholar, Gerhard Lohfink, writes,

> The houses into which the disciples entered were to become bases for the Jesus movement. A net of households into which eschatological peace had entered was to extend throughout the whole land. Everywhere in Israel there were to be people who were captivated by the reign of God and therefore trusted each other to share and care for one another. Thus there would be created a living basis that would support the disciples' work of proclamation.[4]

Although the early disciples knew about the advice that Jethro gave to Moses as recorded in Exodus 18 concerning establishing groups of ten, they primarily established house groups because

---

3. Gehring, p. 53.

4. Gerhard Lohfink, *Does God Need the Church?* (Collegeville, MN: The Liturgical Press, 1998), p. 167.

they were following the house-to-house strategy of their Master given to them as recorded in Luke 9 and 10.

INSIDE A NEW TESTAMENT HOUSE CHURCH

We know that after the Spirit descended at Pentecost, the disciples formed house churches, modeling the strategy Jesus had given to them. House-based ministry became so common that throughout the book of Acts, every mention of a local church or of a church meeting, whether for worship or fellowship, is a reference to a church meeting in a home. Men and women, ablaze with the Spirit of God, began to spread the gospel message from house-to-house (Acts 20:20). House churches played an essential role in the rapid growth and ultimate triumph of Christianity, and it would be safe to say that the first three centuries belonged to the house church movement.

The activity in the house church was diverse and spontaneous but always centered around belief in the risen Jesus. We know they broke bread together, following their master's instructions to remember his death and resurrection (e.g., Luke 22:7-38). Well-known commentator William Barclay writes, "The Lord's Supper began as a family meal or a meal of friends in a private house . . . It was there that the Lord's Supper was born in the church. It was like the Jewish Passover which is a family festival at which the father and the head of the household is the celebrant."[5] Everyone brought food and shared it. They remembered Christ's death on the cross, looking forward to his second coming and the marriage feast of the Lamb (Acts 2:46;

---

5. William Barclay, *The Lord's Supper* (SCM: London, 1967), p. 101, as quoted in Robert and Julia Banks, *The Church Comes Home: A New Base for Community and Mission* (Australia: Albatross Books, 1986), p. 59.

1 Corinthians 11:20-26).[6] Did they celebrate the Lord's Supper every time they met together? We don't know for certain, but we do know it was a very common practice.

Beyond sharing the Lord's Supper together, the agenda for house church meetings was flexible. Paul wrote to the house church in Colossae, "Let the word of Christ dwell in you richly as you teach and admonish one another with all wisdom, and as you sing psalms, hymns and spiritual songs with gratitude in your hearts to God" (Colossians 3:16). Paul wanted the house church believers to encourage one another, share transparently, and to rejoice in God's goodness. We don't see a rigid agenda. Rather, the meeting was a time to minister to one another and meet needs.

The writer of Hebrews gives us a glimpse of the activity in those early house church meetings, "Let us hold unswervingly to the hope we profess, for he who promised is faithful. And let us consider how we may spur one another on toward love and good deeds. Let us not give up meeting together, as some are in the habit of doing, but let us encourage one another—and all the more as you see the Day approaching" (Hebrews 10:23-25). The Holy Spirit transformed each member into an instrument of encouragement and mutual edification.

The members enjoyed each other's presence, laughed together, and drew near to Jesus together. Robert Banks writes, "We find no suggestion that these meetings were conducted with the kind of solemnity and formality that surrounds most weekly Christian gatherings today."[7]

---

6. Lohfink, pp. 147-148.

7. Robert and Julia Banks, *The Church Comes Home: A New Base for Community and Mission* (Australia: Albatross Books, 1986), p. 39.

The early church saw itself as God's new family. Their intense familial love permeated the meetings. As brothers and sisters in Christ's new family, they wanted to serve one another as Jesus served his own disciples. This is why the phrase one another appears more than fifty times in the New Testament. These phrases instructed the early believers on how to cultivate relationships among themselves.

Paul taught the early house churches that each member had an essential role according to his or her giftedness (1 Corinthians 12-14; Romans 12; Ephesians 4). He placed a high emphasis on participation because each person had a contribution to make. When writing to the Corinthian house church, Paul says, "When you come together, everyone has a hymn, or a word of instruction, a revelation, a tongue or an interpretation. All of these must be done for the strengthening of the church" (1 Corinthians 14:26). Paul assumed that they would energetically minister to each other. His concern was that "Everything should be done in a fitting and orderly way" (1 Corinthians 14:40). Ritva Williams writes, "The central activity of the *ekklesia* seems to have been a meal—the Lord's Supper—followed by acts of prophecy, teaching, healing, and speaking in tongues (1 Corinthians 11-14)."[8]

We know that the early churches prayed together. After Peter was supernaturally released from prison, we read in Acts 12:12, "He went to the house of Mary the mother of John, also called Mark, where many people had gathered and were praying." They specifically were praying for Peter to be released from prison,

---

8. Ritva H. Williams, *Stewards, Prophets, Keepers of the Word* (Peabody, MA: Hendrickson Publishers, 2006), p. 17.

but we can assume that prayer characterized the house church meetings. Most scholars agree that the early house churches emphasized the following elements:[9]

- Worship
- Practice of the spiritual gifts
- Teaching
- Prayer
- Fellowship
- Evangelism
- The Lord's Supper
- Baptism

Luke describes homes being used for prayer meetings (Acts 12:12); for an evening of Christian fellowship (Acts 21:7); for holy communion services (Acts 2:46); for a whole night of prayer, worship, and instruction (Acts 20:7); for impromptu evangelistic gatherings (Acts 16:32); for planned meetings to hear the gospel (Acts 10:22); for following up (Acts 18:26); and for organized instruction (Acts 5:42).[10]

Communicating information was another essential activity in the early house churches. News from visitors, sending of letters from one city to another (e.g., Paul's letters, 2 and 3 John), warnings of persecution, and accounts of actual persecutions were all important types of information that passed through the house churches.[11] The house churches also served

9. Gehring, p. 27.

10. Michael Green, *Evangelism in the Early Church* (Grand Rapids, MI: Eerdmans, 2003), Kindle locations 3776-3778.

11. Osiek, MacDonald, Tulloch, p. 14.

as centers of social services for those members who were in need. Young widows and the poorer family members looked to the house churches as a means of support. Apparently, there were some attempts by families to avoid their own responsibilities (1 Timothy 5:4, 5, 8, 16).[12]

HOUSE CHURCH NETWORKS

House churches in the New Testament were not independent of each other. Rather, they were part of a larger unit. The house church and the larger gathering of several house churches existed side by side in early Christianity. In other words, individual believers and house churches considered themselves part of a greater citywide church. Gehring writes,

> The proof of a plurality of house churches alongside the whole church at one location would shed light on the controversial issue regarding the clarification of the relationship between the individual churches and the whole local church, and between the local church and the universal church.[13]

Paul specifically says that he taught publically and from house-to-house (Acts 20:20). In 1 Corinthians 16:19 Paul says, "The churches in the province of Asia send you greetings. Aquila and Priscilla greet you warmly in the Lord, and so does the church that meets at their house." The larger group gathering is seen in Paul's greeting from all the churches in Asia, but then he specifically mentions the house church of Aquila and Priscilla and their particular greetings to the churches. In other words, there were Christians in Ephesus who did not meet at

12. Ibid., p. 14.

13. Gehring, p. 26.

Priscilla and Aquila's home. The evidence points to a plurality of house churches there.

At times the whole church gathered in unidentified places for public ministry. In Acts 15:4, Luke writes, "When they came to Jerusalem, they were welcomed by the church and the apostles and elders, to whom they reported everything God had done through them." Later on in Acts 15:22 we read, "Then the apostles and elders, with the whole church, decided to choose some of their own men and send them to Antioch with Paul and Barnabas." The individual house churches were linked by leadership that occasionally gathered the house churches together. Writing about this leadership link, Ken Giles says,

> It is often assumed that in the New Testament age there were no institutional structures linking individual congregations or local churches to the wider Christian community, but this is not true. The institutional forms that were needed and were appropriate for this period began to appear very early. In the Book of Acts, Luke maintains that a group of elders with general oversight of the Christian community in Jerusalem was in place by the time the church at Antioch was established.[14]

In the Jerusalem church, those leadership associations were especially clear because we read, "Day after day, in the temple courts and from house-to-house, they never stopped teaching and proclaiming the good news that Jesus is the Christ" (Acts 5:42). In the Jerusalem church, the apostolic leadership gathered together the various house churches.

---

14. Giles, 1995, p. 188.

Acts 2:46-47 says, "Every day they continued to meet together in the temple courts. They broke bread in their homes and ate together with glad and sincere hearts, praising God and enjoying the favor of all the people. And the Lord added to their number daily those who were being saved." We see here both the house church meetings as well as those house churches coming together to hear the apostles teaching. Gehring writes,

> The primitive church gathered for two different types of worship services, which can be distinguished from one another on the basis not only of their locality but of their organizational arrangement as well. The main emphasis in the house was on bread breaking. The first Christians likely took part in the temple prayers held in the temple courts, and from there they went into the hall of Solomon for a gathering of the whole congregation, with the emphasis on missionary proclamation and biblical instruction.[15]

The house sizes differed, and we really don't know how many house churches existed in the Jerusalem area.[16] We only know that they came together under the leadership of the apostles to hear the apostles' teaching and to celebrate the resurrected Christ, just like Acts 5:42 says. David Shenk and Irvin Stutzman break down the early church activity further,

---

15. Gehring, pp. 81-82.

16. I give a more detailed description of the size of the early house churches in my book, *Biblical Foundations for the Cell-based Church* (pp. 92-95). After detailing the physical sizes of the early church homes and apartments, I concluded that most early house churches would not have had more than fifteen or twenty people. I also cite various scholars and historians who have reached similar conclusions.

> The first congregations were house churches which met in small clusters throughout the Jerusalem metropolitan area. Since most of the homes in the Jerusalem area were small, we may assume that from ten to twenty people gathered in each of these cell group fellowships. Probably 100-200 of these small congregations, meeting in living rooms throughout the Jerusalem area, were formed within days of Pentecost. Yet they never functioned independently of each other. These home cell groups formed the clusters comprising the church in Jerusalem, a congregation who for some time met around the temple area for celebration events.[17]

We also see the whole church coming together in Corinth. Paul says, "So if the whole church comes together and everyone speaks in tongues, and some who do not understand or some unbelievers come in, will they not say that you are out of your mind?" (1 Corinthians 14:23). Paul implies that at other times the Christians in Corinth met separately in smaller house churches. Yet, both were considered the *church*. Arthur G. Patzia, senior professor of New Testament at Fuller Seminary, writes,

> Paul's reference to "the church of God in Corinth" (1 Corinthians 1:2) and to the believers coming together "as a church" (1 Corinthians 11:18), along with the implication that Gaius was hosting the entire *(holes)* church (Romans 16:23), suggest that there were occasions in Corinth when all the believers assembled. In time, these letters were shared with other churches

---

17. David W. Shenk and Ervin R. Stutzman, *Creating Communities of the Kingdom: New Testament Models of Church Planting* (Scottdale, PA: Herald Press, 1988), p. 92.

> in the city and read at their worship services before a redactor collected and edited them into their current format as 1 and 2 Corinthians.[18]

Paul addressed the whole congregation in a particular place as *church* and also used the same word *church* to describe the individual house groups (1 Corinthians 1:1; 16:19). The one was not seen as detracting from the status of the other. Wherever believers met together, they were "the church of God." James Dunn writes,

> The implication of 1 Cor. 16:19 set alongside 14:23 (referring to the whole church meeting together) is probably that church gatherings consisted of more regular small house groups interspersed with less frequent (weekly, monthly?) gatherings of the 'the whole church.'"[19]

If there were five hundred thousand believers by the end of the first century, as some have suggested, there must have been countless house churches. God crafted a strategy for growth that included use of the believer's home property for the early meetings. Only those transformed by the gospel's message would risk opening their homes. Yet, all who did exemplified God's love and power for their neighbors and friends to see and experience. In the process, many more were converted, and the early church continued to spread from house-to-house.

---

18. Arthur Patzia, *The Emergence of the Church: Context, Growth,* Leadership and Worship (Downers Grove, IL: InterVarsity, 2001), p. 192.

19. James D.G. Dunn, *The Theology of Paul the Apostle* (Grand Rapids, MI: Eerdmans, 1998), p. 541.

LESSONS LEARNED

- Jesus chose to establish the first churches in houses, knowing that his message needed to first penetrate families.
- After Pentecost, Christ's disciples continued house-to-house ministry. In the small house atmosphere, disciples were formed and lives were changed.
- Networked house churches or cell churches were the normal type of church in the first century. The early church never owned a building until approximately two hundred years after Christ's death.
- The house churches were networked together. The writers of the New Testament used *ecclesia* (church) to describe both the individual house church gatherings as well as the larger gatherings of house churches. Both types of gathering were equally recognized as the Church of Jesus Christ.

Chapter 2

THE DEMISE OF THE HOUSE CHURCH

On October 28, 312, Constantine faced Maxentius, who was then in control of Rome. Constantine was convinced that he needed more powerful aid than his military forces could provide, especially since soldiers in the armies of Maxentius outnumbered his own four to one. He looked for divine help but struggled to select which god to choose from among the wide variety of Greek and Roman gods.

It occurred to him that, of the many emperors who had preceded him, those who had put their hope in a multitude of gods and served them with sacrifices and offerings had been deceived by flattering predictions and oracles that did not come true.

While he was pondering this dilemma, an extraordinary sign appeared to him from heaven. Constantine reported having seen a cross of light, bearing the inscription, "By this symbol you will conquer." He was struck with amazement by the sight, and while he pondered this, night came. In his sleep, Christ appeared to him with the same cross and commanded him to make a likeness of that sign as a safeguard in all engagements with his enemies.

He was amazed at the vision and resolved to worship no other God than the one who had appeared to him. He sent for the followers of Jesus to explain to him what the vision meant. They told Constantine that the cross which had appeared was Christ's victory over death. They told him about Christ's birth and incarnation. Constantine was in awe of the divine manifestation he had seen.

The next day, the two armies clashed, and Constantine won a decisive victory, even though he was greatly outnumbered. This event changed Constantine's life. From that time forth, he promoted Christianity as the one true religion.

While historians still debate whether he was devoted to Christianity for political purposes or from heartfelt conviction, we do know that Constantine's promotion of Christianity changed the course of history. He made the priests his advisers and invited God's ministers to spend time with him. He showered them with every possible honor, treating them as dignitaries and allowing certain Christians to join him at his table. They accompanied him on his travels, believing that the God they served would help him in battle. He gave vast amounts of money from his own personal treasury to build churches and to decorate their sanctuaries.

LEGALIZATION OF CHRISTIANITY

Until Constantine rose to power (312 AD), the Christian church faced periods of fiery persecution. The first documented case began with Nero (37-68 AD), who blamed the 64 AD fire in Rome on the Christians. By the mid-second century, mobs would often stone Christians.

The first empire-wide persecution took place under Maximinus Thrax (173–238 AD), which targeted the clergy. Under the emperor Decius (201–251 AD), a persecution of Christian lay people spread across the empire. Everyone had to offer a public sacrifice to the emperor as the only true god and then receive written certificates of doing it. Decius then authorized roving commissions to ensure his decrees were carried out. Those who didn't obey faced arrest, imprisonment, torture, and even execution.

The persecutions culminated in what is known as the great persecution in the third and fourth century. It began with a series of four edicts banning Christian practices and ordering the imprisonment of Christian clergy. The persecution intensified until all Christians in the empire were commanded to sacrifice to the gods or face immediate execution. Over twenty thousand Christians died during Diocletian's reign (245–311 AD).

But then Constantine came to power in 312 AD and legalized Christianity. Constantine promised to forgo persecution and make Christianity the state religion. The old order was suddenly reversed. Christianity became the favored, dominant religion.

Those who were not Christians were expected to submit to the savior and the state. In a very group-oriented society, it was the norm to conform, and so people did.

While many truly converted, others conformed in name only. They said yes with their mouths, but not with their hearts. Historian Joseph Lynch writes,

> The conversion of the Emperor Constantine was a major turning point in the history of Christianity. In one lifetime, the Christian church moved from a position of illegality and ferocious persecution to one of favor. The church historian Eusebius of Caesarea (c. 260-339) had been imprisoned during the persecution of Diocletian and had seen friends, including his beloved teacher, killed. Yet, in his later years he was a personal acquaintance and occasional guest of the Emperor Constantine. The church moved rapidly from being an association of outsiders to taking a central position in Roman society.[1]

Constantine hoped Christianity would be a unifying force, so he rewarded those who joined the church and ensured that the Roman Empire became intimately entwined with its affairs. As a result, the church inherited great sums of wealth and had a privileged position in society. Constantine built impressive churches at the holy sites of Christianity.[2] Large, sacred buildings became more esteemed than intimate home fellowships.[3]

---

1. Joseph Lynch, *The Medieval Church: A Brief History* (London: Longman Group UK Limited, 1992), p. 10.

2. Ibid., p. 16.

3. Jim and Carol Plueddemann, *Pilgrims in Progress* (Wheaton, IL: Harold Shaw Publishers, 1990), p. 4.

Constantine publicly acknowledged and recompensed certain leaders who could trace their lineage back to the apostles. The church began to esteem this type of *inheritance* more than spiritual gifting and piety. In major cities, bishops began to grow in power. Their word was respected and obeyed.

FROM SIMPLE TO RITUALISTIC

With the rise of Constantine, house churches were no longer the primary meeting place for believers. There was little interaction between the priests and the people, and the church became progressively ritualistic. The Eucharist replaced the individual sharing, so common in the early house churches. The early New Testament believers celebrated the Lord's Supper as a meal, but by the second century it had become a ritual. Rather than exercising spiritual gifts in an atmosphere conducive to ministry, people came to the mass, performed Christian rituals, and left without the spiritual and emotional intimacy they once had with other believers in the house churches.

When Christianity was a despised, foreign religion, only the true believers participated in the affairs of the church. Now, everyone embraced Christianity. Whole armies were baptized. People converted from the pagan religions to Christianity because it was the culturally, acceptable thing to do. The world became part of the church, and the church became part of the world. Before in the lowly house churches, everyone was expected to become a disciple and live out the Christian faith. With the rise of Constantine and the legalization of Christianity, the church eroded from the inside out.

SMALL GROUPS AMONG THE CLERGY

Although there is no record that small group structures were established to care for the burgeoning needs of the growing congregations, we do know that there were small groups among the clergy. Ambrose, the bishop of Milan (339-397 AD) lived during the time of Constantine, and he and his colleagues resorted to small groups to fill their own spiritual needs.

Apparently, several early church fathers, like Ambrose, found a tremendous amount of strength in small community interaction. St. Augustine of Hippo, for example, was significantly influenced by these small groups under Ambrose. These small groups did not extend to the laity because lay participation was not encouraged at that time. As Herbert T. Mayer writes, "This was the common pattern for centuries: the real strength and vitality of the church lay in the small groups of clergy gathered around a cathedral and the bishop or in the small group of monks gathered around a strong and influential leader."[4]

HIERARCHICAL LEADERSHIP

In the New Testament letters, leadership hierarchy does not exist. The words bishop, pastor, and elder are interchangeable and point to the same role. A *bishop/overseer* was also called a *pastor/shepherd* and a *presbyter/elder*, since all three terms in the Greek address the same group of people in Acts 20:17, 28 and 1 Peter 5:1-5. Most likely these titles represented house church leaders or overseers of various house churches. Writing about these leadership roles, Gehring says,

---

4. Herbert T. Mayer, "Pastoral Roles and Mission Goals," *Currents in Theology and Missions*, Vol. 3 (Chicago, IL: Lutheran School of Theology, 1976), p. 298.

> Everything seems to indicate that they were overseers of the churches that met in their homes, much like Stephanas in Corinth; in other words, they were leaders of individual house churches. Together as a group such overseers could have formed the leadership team or council for the whole local church in that city.[5]

The house churches were the breeding ground for leadership in the early church, and the early bishops led local house churches and also functioned in the role of supervisors. Arthur G. Patzia writes, "Bishops were overseers of local house churches and were assisted by a group of individuals identified as deacons."[6] But everything changed with Constantine. He placed priests on government salary and encouraged a hierarchical view of leadership. The people looked to the clergy and special saints for revelation and direction.

A GRADUAL DRIFT

Although the change from simple house church leadership to the vast-reaching authority of the bishops culminated in the rise of Constantine, the actual shift was very gradual and almost imperceptible. This shift began in the second century when the people were clamoring for authority because of false religions and cults. With the growing heresy of Gnosticism and numerous cults spreading rapidly, people looked for an authoritative Christian voice. Those who appeared to have more authority were those who could demonstrate that their lineage was directly linked to the apostle Peter. This linkage gave certain people unprecedented authority and credibility. Irenaeus (130-202 AD) was one of the first Church fathers to

---

5. Gehring, p. 206.

6. Patzia, p. 171.

promote the succession of certain apostles. The church historian Kenneth Scott Latourette explains,

> He [Irenaeus] . . . was emphatic that the apostles had appointed as successors bishops to whom they had committed the churches. . . . These bishops had been followed by others in unbroken line who were also guardians and guarantors of the apostolic teaching. He hints that he could, if there were space, give the lists of the bishops of all the churches, but he singles out that of the Church of Rome . . .[7]

Because only a few could actually trace their lineage to the apostle Peter, those who could became responsible for larger and larger groups of believers.[8] Gérald Vallée writes,

> Gradually the bishop became the chief officer of the local congregation and was called "priest," while the elders were seen to share in the bishop's ministry and to conduct the liturgy with a teaching/preaching function; later they were also to be called priests. The bishop appointed or ordained deacons and elders by the laying on of hands, signifying the bestowing of a spiritual power in a hierarchical society.

Some early church fathers, like Tertullian (160-220 AD), resisted the idea of giving special authority to those who could show their linkage with past apostles. Tertullian promoted the priesthood of all believers and opposed the growing tendency

---

7. Kenneth Scott Latourette, *A History of Christianity*, Vols. 1 and 2 (New York: Harper & Row Publishers, 1975), p. 131.

8. Osiek and Balch, p. 35.

toward hierarchical authority.[9] Yet, his voice was drowned out as the people clamored for leadership.

By the third century, this line of succession, along with the distinct church offices, had become quite developed in the Church.[10] In major cities, bishops grew in power, evolving into patriarchs and popes. Their word became the word of God. They were the ones who established correct doctrine and condemned those who did not agree. By the fourth century celibacy became a requirement for priests and bishops to demonstrate dedication to their task. The church progressed from the family of God meeting in homes to institutionalized religion. The Church turned from simplicity and grew in complexity. The authors of *Home Cell Groups and House Churches* write,

> For generations after the apostles, the church continued its spontaneous lay (people of God) witness in the cities and along the great trade routes of the empire. However, some ideological changes were taking place, which were altering the New Testament theology of the church. The plurality and equality of leadership was giving way to a hierarchical arrangement with bishops becoming the central figure followed by the presbyters (who later became priests) and deacons. Later such roles as exorcists and acolytes were added.

---

9. George Huntston Williams, Frank Forrester Church, Timothy Francis George, *Continuity and Discontinuity in Church History: Essays Presented to George Huntston Williams on the Occasion of His 65th Birthday* (Boston, MA: Brill Publishing: 1979) pp. 59-60.

10. Some of the background material used in this chapter was derived from the lectures of Dr. Rosell, 1995 lecturer at Columbia International University. Rosell's course on early church history covered the time period from the birth of the Church to Luther and the Reformation.

> It appears that after the apostles, the bishops, who were at first pastors, assumed a role of authority as well as leadership. The bishop would have been pastor of a house church; but in time his congregation came to be the central one, and the other house congregations in a given city would then be pastored by presbyters under the authority of the bishop. In a given city, certainly in the Western church, only one pastor in a city could be a bishop.[11]

The Church moved from bishop as a servant-shepherd caring for a house church or group of house churches to an administrative ruler. The spontaneity that was once so present in the local house churches came under strict control of the elected bishops.[12]

PASSIVITY ENCOURAGED

Passivity became the norm as the years went passed. Historian Richard Vallée writes, "The distinction between clergy (bishops and priests) and laity became strongly emphasized, whereby exclusive authority was given to the office of the bishop (all at once priest, prophet, and teacher), the laity being reduced to a passive role."[13] William Brown writes about this passivity,

---

11. C. Kirk Hadaway, Francis M. DuBose, Stuart A. Wright, *Home Cell Groups and House Churches* (Nashville, TN: Broadman Press, 1987), pp. 69-70.

12. Garth Rosell, *Birth of the Church to the Reformation*, graduate level series of 24 tapes & notes (Columbia, South Carolina, Columbia International University, 1995), tape 5.

13. Gérard Valleé, *The Shaping of Christianity: The History and Literature of Its Formative Centuries (100-800)* (Mahwah, New Jersey: Paulist Press, 1999), p. 132.

> . . . the reversion to an "official" priesthood or ministry . . . cast the laity chiefly into the role of hearers of the Law and spectators of the mysterious tableau of the sacrifices. This passive role in worship became once more the normal experience of the people of God as the church developed.[14]

The church's outward structure reflected the civil administrative geography, often using the very same terminology for its organization (e.g., *dioceses*, *vicars*).[15] Ministry became the exclusive, personal role of select ministers and the rest were reduced to the hearer role. The normal Christian was expected to obey. The Bible was taken from the hands of the people and given to those learned men who would study it and offer their judgments. This cast system of hierarchy killed lay initiative. Personal innovation and freedom were discouraged. Submission and obedience were encouraged. As the hierarchy grew in strength, torturous methods were used to prevent lay people from expounding on their biblical ideas.

When the house church structure was functioning properly, there was liberty for the laity to minister. The priesthood of all believers was in full force and the needs of the church were being met. Yet as Church history continued, the rights of particular office-holders usurped those of the common lay ministers.[16] Many lay people, however, were so dissatisfied by the church structures and hierarchy that they decided to

---

14. William Brown, *Growing the Church through Small Groups in the Australian Context,* D.Min. dissertation, (Pasadena, CA: Fuller Theological Seminary, 1992), p. 37.

15. Valleé, p. 132.

16. Paul Johnson, *A History of Christianity* (New York: Atheneum Press, 1976), p. 81.

reform the church by creating a new structure of their own, as we will see in the next chapter.

LESSONS LEARNED

- Beginning in the second century, there was a gradual tendency toward hierarchy, which blossomed into its fullest expression under Constantine. The shift toward placing authority in the hands of a few was a slow, gradual change.
- Constantine created the first state church that honored those who could trace their lineage to Peter. During the time of Constantine, religious rituals, symbols, and elaborate cathedrals were common.
- The hierarchical view of the church separated the work of the clergy from the laity, which resulted in passivity among the laity.
- Early church history shows a tendency to remove ministry from ordinary lay people and place it in the hands of a few—which ultimately stunts the development of the priesthood of all believers and the free-flow of the gifts of the Spirit.

Chapter 3

SMALL GROUPS AND MONASTICISM

Saint Anthony the Great (251-356 AD), also called "star of the wilderness" was certainly not the first Christian to leave the cities for a life of solitude. But he was probably the most famous because of his austere and rigorous Christian spirituality, which he spread to Palestine, Syria, Greece, and across the Mediterranean Sea to Italy. It all started when he headed out into the desert region of North Africa, some sixty miles west of Alexandria, Egypt.

According to Athanasius, an early church father, the devil fought Saint Anthony by afflicting him with boredom, laziness, and phantoms of women, which he overcame by the power of prayer. After that, he moved to a tomb, where he closed the door on himself and depended on local villagers to bring him food. When the devil perceived his ascetic life and his intense worship, he was envious and beat him mercilessly, leaving him unconscious. When his friends from the local village came to visit Anthony and found him in this condition, they carried him to a church.

After he recovered, he made a second effort and went back to the desert where he lived strictly enclosed in an old abandoned Roman fort for some twenty years. According to Athanasius, the devil again resumed his war against Anthony, only this time the phantoms were in the form of wild beasts, wolves, lions, snakes and scorpions. They appeared as if they were about to attack him or cut him into pieces. But the saint would laugh at them and say, "If any of you have any authority over me, only one would have been sufficient to fight me." With these words, they disappeared, and God gave him the victory over the devils.

While in the fort, he only communicated with the outside world by a crevice through which food would be passed and he would say a few words. He did not allow anyone to enter his cell. Whoever came to him, stood outside and listened to his advice.

Then one day he emerged from the fort. By this time, most had expected him to have wasted away, or gone insane in his solitary confinement, but he emerged healthy, serene, and enlightened. Everyone was amazed that he had been through these trials and emerged spiritually rejuvenated. He was hailed as a hero, and from this time forth the legend of Anthony began to spread and grow.[1]

Many followed the example of Anthony and became known as monks. The word monk means *alone* (from Greek *monos* = alone, solitary) and by definition, a monk lived apart from others. Saint Anthony's example stirred many to seek God alone, but eventually monks decided they would be more effective by gathering together into monasteries for fellowship and protection. Although Saint Anthony's story is one of the earliest and most famous, all monks had one thing in common: the desire for a sacrificial, second level commitment to Jesus Christ that went beyond the status quo.

RESISTING THE STATUS QUO

Those who chose the monastic way of life renounced worldly pursuits and devoted themselves fully to God's work. Monks were willing to deny themselves and live by established spiritual norms that went beyond the religious requirements for lay people and other spiritual leaders.

The monks resisted the lavish gains of the church under Constantine. They realized that the church's political gains were sinking the cause of Christ. They viewed the church as lukewarm and compromised with the world. Joseph Lynch writes, "Some of them, mostly men, abandoned urban life and ordinary careers and sought remote places, where they lived lives

1. Athanasius Jerome Sulpicius Severus Gregory The Great, *Early Christian Lives,* trans. Carolinne White (Penguin Classics: New York 1998), pp. 1-70.

of systematic and severe self-denial, coupled with prayer and meditation on the Scriptures. These were the first monks."[2]

Many of these lay monks were drawn to a life of isolationism in order to pursue their own salvation. They kept entirely to themselves. Judith Herrin writes,

> While this organized and most visible feature of Christianity continued to grow, a quite different form of expansion was under way in the countryside, in the wildest and most deserted parts of the empire, furthest away from urban civilization. It sprang from a desire to shun the world and all its evils, to escape to the desert and commune with God alone. The practice had older pre-Christian roots, which were taken over by Christians seeking to live by Christ's command: "leave all thou hast and follow me."[3]

They went out into the desert or wilderness to seek God alone, to deny the pleasure of marriage, and to practice extreme asceticism. This total withdrawal became quite common by the close of the third century. However, the balance between individual isolation and Christian community began to occur. We know that from 300 to 700 AD many monks gathered together to practice the life of self-denial. Part of the reason why these isolated individuals couldn't practice their faith alone was the repeated hostile attacks by pagan forces, both near Rome and in Africa. Some of the monasteries even built defenses to keep out the intruders.[4]

---

2. Lynch, p. 18.

3. Judith Herrin, *The Formation of Christendom* (Princeton, New Jersey: Princeton University Press, 1987), p. 59.

4. Ibid., p. 71.

DISCOVERING THE NEED FOR COMMUNITY

Many of the monks formed monasteries on the edges of the cities in order to avoid isolationism. These monks connected a relationship with God with the need to relate to other believers.[5] For example, Basil (329-379 AD) established a monastery in Asia Minor where brotherly love and care was promoted. Brown writes,

> Gradually some of these hermits discovered that if they grouped together in small communities, they experienced spiritual as well as practical benefits. In time many of the features of the Christian community in Acts 2 were reincorporated into monastic life, and yet there was still a separation from the people.[6]

Even when living together, chastity and obedience were strictly practiced. Restrictions were placed on diet and hard work was required.

Some monasteries asked for a lifetime commitment while others, like Celtic monasticism, practiced *permeability*. That is, people were able to move freely in and out of the monastic system at different points of life. Young boys and girls would enter the system to pursue Latin scholarship. Students would sometimes travel from faraway lands to enter the Irish monasteries. When these students became adults, they would leave the monastery to live out their lives. Eventually, these people would retire back to a secure community provided by the monastery and stay until their death. However, some would stay long-term within the monastery and become leaders.

5. Brian Patrick McGuire, *Friendship and Community* (London: Cornwell University Press, 2010), pp. 38-60.

6. Brown, p. 37.

Permeable monasticism popularized the use of the vernacular and helped mesh the norms of the secular and religious, unlike other parts of Europe where monasteries were more isolated.

Most monasteries developed their own rules and strategies, along with their customs and traditions. [7] However, the rule of Saint Benedict became increasingly adopted by monasteries because of the way it balanced the spiritual disciplines, work, and community.[8] The rule of Saint Benedict is a collection of precepts written by Saint Benedict of Nursia (480–547 AD) for monks living communally under the authority of a spiritual leader called an abbot. During the one thousand five hundred years of its existence, it became the leading guide in western Christianity for monastic living in community. The two key principles of Saint Benedict's Rule are:

1. Peace (*pax*)
2. Pray and work (*Ora et labora*)

Compared to other monastic orders, the Rule of Saint Benedict provided a moderate path between individual zeal and institutionalism. Because of this middle ground, it became widely popular. Benedict's concerns were the needs of monks in a community environment, to establish order, to foster an understanding of the relational nature of human beings, and to provide a spiritual father to support and strengthen the person's spiritual growth. It organized the monastic day into regular periods of communal and private prayer, sleep, spiritual

---

7. Edward A. Wynne, *Traditional Catholic Religious Orders* (Oxford, UK: Transaction Books, 1988), p. 24.

8. David Knowles, *Christian Monasticism* (New York: World University Library, 1977), p. 40.

reading, and manual labor. In later centuries, intellectual work and teaching took the place of farming, crafts, or other forms of manual labor.

MONASTICISM AND MISSIONS

Patrick was born around 385 AD in Roman Britain, a province of the Roman Empire from 43 to 409 AD. As a boy of fourteen, he was captured during a raiding party and taken to Ireland as a slave to herd and tend sheep. Ireland at that time was a land of Druids and pagans. Patrick learned the language and practices of the people who held him captive. During this time, he turned to God in prayer, and God revealed himself. Patrick wrote,

> The love of God and his fear grew in me more and more, as did the faith, and my soul was roused, so that, in a single day, I have said as many as a hundred prayers and in the night, nearly the same. I prayed in the woods and on the mountain, even before dawn. I felt no hurt from the snow or ice or rain.[9]

Patrick's captivity lasted until he was twenty. He then escaped after God showed him in a dream to leave Ireland by going to the coast. There he found some sailors who took him back to Britain, where he reunited with his family. He then had another dream in which the people of Ireland were calling out to him saying, "We beg you, holy youth, to come and walk among us once more."

---

9. Quoted in an article called "St Patrick," Catholic Online, Accessed at http://www.catholic.org/saints/saint.php?saint_id=89 on Tuesday, April 1, 2014.

Before going back to Ireland, he studied for the priesthood, was ordained as a bishop by Saint Germanus around 430 AD, and was then officially sent to establish Christ's church in Ireland. He arrived in Ireland on March 25, 433 AD. One legend says that he met a chieftain of one of the tribes, who tried to kill Patrick. Later this chieftain, Dichu, was converted after he was unable to move his arm until he became friendly to Patrick.

Patrick began preaching the gospel throughout Ireland, converting many. He and his disciples preached, made disciples, and planted churches all over the country. Kings, their families, and entire kingdoms converted to Christianity when hearing Patrick's message. God performed many miracles through Patrick, and he wrote about God's power and love in his autobiography called *Confession of Saint Patrick*.

Patrick's model of reaching out to others was highly relational, hospitable, and community-oriented. He and his followers would move into a pagan area and then become part of the community. They took seriously the passage in the book of Psalms that says, "Taste and see that the LORD is good; blessed is the man who takes refuge in him" (34:8). Patrick believed that the truth is first caught and then taught, so they tried to make the church accessible to the people.

They modeled what they wanted others to follow. They lived life in community, but this was never an end in itself. They never lost sight of giving their community away. In fact, their evangelistic strategy resembled the prayer of Jesus in John 17 where he tells the disciples that the world would know and believe by their unity. Patrick's band of believers talked a lot about the love and unity within the Trinity and used the three-sided shamrock to explain the Trinity. They would then demonstrate the love of the Trinity in their communities. The evangelistic bands knew their own lives needed to reflect God's character if they were going to win the unreached Irish.

Those who entered the group saw transformed lives, love in action, and how disciples were supposed to act. The seekers were then invited to become Christ's disciples. As a result of this strategy, many received Jesus, new groups multiplied, and missionary bands infiltrated unreached areas. The discipleship and the outreach were intimately connected together.

Inspired by Patrick's model, waves of missionary bands were sent out over the continent. A community of monks (ten to twelve) would settle in a non-Christian area and establish a Christian church. They would preach until a number were converted, and then they would teach the new converts. Once they had established the church, they would leave to go to another part of Europe, believing their purpose was to establish the monastic community throughout the land.

Using the same small group strategy, Columban and twelve companions went to Gaul (modern day France) around 590 AD. They preached and taught, living with any who shared hospitality with them.[10] Columban was so successful that he started three monasteries and continued to work with the uncivilized barbarians, trying to convert them to Christianity. This went against the practice of the local bishops, who preferred to stay in the larger towns and cities. The bishops summoned Columban to curtail his activity, but he refused;

10. As quoted in Paul Pierson, *Historical Development of the Christian Movement,* MH520 study notes for doctoral admission (Pasadena, CA: Fuller Theological Seminary, School of World Mission, 1989), p. 11.

instead, he sent them a letter in which he told them that they weren't doing their jobs. Columban felt a bishop should live in the countryside and reach the pagans.

The Celtic spirit of evangelism and missions continued with such men as Bernard of Clairvaux (1090-1153), Saint Dominic (1170-1221), and Saint Francis of Assisi (1181-1226). These men were dedicated saints who followed hard after God, as they understood him.[11] The early monastic missionary bands were very similar to evangelism in the early church, where neighbors could see and hear what was happening in the house churches. Speaking of the inner drive that motivated these Celtic missionaries, Hardinge writes,

> Individual response to a divinely placed inner drive to spread their faith, singly or in groups, impelled Celtic missionaries to go forth. Without credentials or material support, self-reliant and trusting in God, they accomplished more than their numbers would warrant. Spontaneity, lack of traditionalism, and individuality were the features of this movement.[12]

For the most part, Monasticism was a purifying element to the Roman Catholic Church, as well as a powerful evangelistic outreach. It did not, however, bridge the gap between the laity and the clergy. The clergy continued to have their own small groups, while the monastic lay movement met separately. Brown writes,

> At first this movement developed quite apart from the clergy dominated Catholic Church. In fact, it was

---

11. Brown, p. 37.

12. As quoted in Pierson, p. 10.

> looked down upon by those in authority. Yet, by the end of the fifth century, monasticism had become so extensive that it became characteristic of the Catholic Church.[13]

One of the Monastic groups that tried to reform the church, met in houses, and had a significant impact during its time was a movement called the Brethren of the Common Life.

BRETHREN OF THE COMMON LIFE

This monastic movement originated in the Netherlands under the leadership of Gerard Groote (1340-1384). Groote was born during a time of papal crisis in which there were two reigning popes and eventually three who claimed Peter's throne. Those living in the latter part of the fourteenth century expressed their discontent in literature as well as in rebellion.[14] They wanted economic and spiritual change and sensed a new liberty to communicate through literature. Gerard Groote exemplified this new mood.

Groote became a successful educator. God converted him and stirred him to preach the gospel and live a simple lifestyle. John Neale, who wrote an extensive history of this movement, says, "The first effect of his conversion was his intense zeal to bring back his countrymen to real, vital religion."[15] He spent two years in a monastery but then left to preach the gospel. Groote went from place to place calling men and women to

---

13. Latourette, p. 222.

14. Margaret Aston, *The Fifteenth Century: The Prospect of Europe* (New York: W. W. Norton and Company, 1968), p. 144.

15. John M. Neale, *A History of the So-called Jansenist Church of Holland* (New York: Cosimo Classics, 2007), p. 76.

repentance, proclaiming the beauty of Divine love, and pinpointing the degradation of the clergy. He would often preach three-hour sermons, and the people hung on every word.[16] When the clergy rose up against him, Groote humbly submitted and didn't incite the people against them. In 1380, Groote chose twelve disciples who met regularly with him in a house. He prepared them to preach God's Word. Yet, Groote's disciples were also very intellectual, studying the ancient texts and preparing themselves spiritually.

Members of the clergy even enrolled themselves in his brotherhood, which eventually was approved by the pope. They devoted themselves to doing charitable work, nursing the sick, copying Scripture, and preaching the gospel. They later made extensive use of the printing press to publish their spiritual writings widely. They also obtained qualified teachers for their schools and revived the spiritual and intellectual life of the Catholic Church. Books and learning were central to the communities of the Brethren, whose scrupulous copies of works of piety supported their houses.

When Groote first started, education in the Netherlands was rare. Very few people apart from the clergy had studied at the universities and cathedral schools in Paris or in Cologne, so there were very few scholars in the land. The goal for many was simply to ensure that their children could read and write when graduating from school. Groote and the Brethren of the Common Life determined to change this. They started a number of schools that became famous for their high standards of learning. Many well-known people attended their schools, including Nicholas of Cusa (German philosopher, theologian, jurist, and astronomer), Thomas á Kempis (author of *The*

---

16. Ibid., p. 76.

Imitation of Christ), and Desiderius Erasmus (classical scholar, social critic, teacher, and theologian).

By the year 1475, the movement had expanded to some one hundred houses for women and over thirty men's homes.[17] Each house of the Brethren consisted of four or more priests, along with a few laymen who gathered together voluntarily.[18] The Brethren never took monastic vows, such as the vows or promises of poverty, chastity, and obedience, which were common vows that other monastic orders bound themselves to fulfill. Nor did they ask for or receive alms. Rather they worked for their daily bread. Their chief aim in coming together was to cultivate the inner life, which they accomplished through sharing property and practicing the spiritual disciplines, such as praying and meditating on Scripture.[19]

They tried to live like their neighbors and practiced their communal lifestyle in normal neighborhood houses. They distinguished their lifestyle from their neighbors, not because they were part of a religious order, but simply because they were followers of Jesus. John Van Engen notes, "Brothers or sisters lived on ordinary city streets, walked with people to church and to market, maintained relations with family and friends; and yet lived a life apart in religious practice, in dress, in social structure."[20]

---

17. Kenneth Strand, *A Reformation Paradox* (Ann Arbor, MI: Ann Arbor Publishers, 1960), p. 22.

18. Neale, p. 96.

19. Ibid., p. 97.

20. John Van Engen, "Conversion and Conformity," 50-51. On a middle order in medieval society, see "Appendix: *Mediocres (Mediani, Medii)* inthe Middle Ages," in Giles Constable, *Three Studies in Medieval Religious and*

The Brethren multiplied their houses when there were approximately fifteen to twenty people. Carol Geisler writes,

> As the pious reputation of the Brothers and Sisters spread, the small and unassuming beginning of sixteen poor women living in Geert Grote's house began to develop into a sizeable system of communities. John Brinckerinck, who became rector of Grote's house in 1392, had to turn women away from that first small household due to lack of space, sending them to start foundations in other parts of the city. By 1391, the community of Brothers established by Florens Radewijns had outgrown his vicarage and moved to a larger house. Visitors, impressed by the lifestyle of the Brothers and Sisters, asked for assistance in establishing devout households in their own towns.[21]

They did not call their community a convent or a monastery, but a *domus*, a house.[22] Albert Hyma describes this movement as a ". . . protest against the formalism of the church in the fourteenth century."[23] Because the Brethren didn't operate as an official order, many priests and bishops attacked them. In response, the Brethren wrote, *The Treatise on the Common Life.*

Social Thought (Cambridge: Cambridge University Press, 1995): 342-60 as quoted in Carol Geisler, *An Obedient Defense of Disobedience: The Brothers of the Common Life and the Boundaries of Religion.* Ph.D. dissertation for Concordia, Seminary (Concordia, St. Louis, MO, 2008), p. 37.

21. Carol Geisler, *An Obedient Defense of Disobedience: The Brothers of the Common Life and the Boundaries of Religion.* Ph.D. dissertation for Concordia, Seminary (Concordia, St. Louis, MO, 2008), p. 54.

22. Ibid., p. 187.

23. Albert Hyma, *The Brethren of the Common Life* (Grand Rapids, MI: Eerdmans Publishing Company, 1950), p. 7.

This document points out that the Brethren were just pious men who chose to meet together in private homes, to share all things in common, and to exhort one another.[24] They didn't want to become part of the establishment. They simply wanted to live out the Christian life and follow God wholeheartedly.

LESSONS LEARNED

- Monasticism was a response to formalism and ritualism in the church. The common monastic features were a total commitment to Jesus Christ and the desire to live apart from the world.
- Eventually individual monks felt the need to come together for community, protection, and greater effectiveness.
- Some monastic orders were unbalanced, emphasizing the abstinence from things normally considered good (e.g., marriage, family, sleep,and so forth). The nuclear family was underemphasized in monasticism.
- The Celtic missionary bands were examples of life-giving small groups that evangelized and won people through community outreach. Many followed their example by planting community-oriented, vibrant churches throughout Europe.
- The Brethren of the Common Life was a monastic movement that emphasized spirituality, scholarship, and the preaching God's Word. They met in regular neighborhood homes and started new house communities when the group grew too large.

---

24. Ibid., p. 73.

Chapter 4

SMALL GROUPS DURING THE PRE-REFORMATION

In the twelfth century, canon law governed the people. Everyone was required to obey a complicated set of rules that laid out religious rights, duties, and laws. This canon law became more and more complex as individual popes and bishops would add rules to it, which were then incorporated as part of the official rules for church life. Joseph Lynch writes,

> Already in the sixth century, the accumulation of diverse texts made the canon law complex and even

> contradictory. Here and there scholars attempted to bring order to the canon law by selecting texts and arranging them systematically under topic headings. Such a canonical collection, which might be a single thick volume, was used by a bishop to manage his church.[1]

One of the religious rules forbade people to preach the gospel unless they received explicit approval from the Roman Church authorities. Some preachers didn't obey this rule and paid dearly for it.

Peter Waldo, for example, a prosperous merchant of Lyon, France, felt compelled by God to preach the gospel when he witnessed the sudden death of a well-known citizen and then heard a musician's ballad about the shortness of life. God spoke to him that all that mattered was preparation for heaven, and he became a dedicated follower of Jesus Christ, committed to preaching the gospel everywhere and to everyone.

He had one major problem, though. He lacked permission. The authorities in Lyon told him to stop until he received the official blessing from Rome. Waldo's zeal led him to go to Rome to get that permission.

He and one other follower appeared at the Third Lateran Council of 1179 to request permission from the pope. The special papal committee asked them whether they believed in the persons of the Trinity and they answered, "Yes." And "in the Mother of Christ?" To which they also replied "Yes." The committee burst out laughing at their ignorance, for it was not proper to believe in, but to believe on, Mary. The

---

1. Lynch, p. 68.

committee rejected them as unlearned and ignorant men and forbade them to preach. Waldo and his followers continued to preach the gospel, believing they had authority from heaven.

YEARNING FOR CHANGE

Other unauthorized preachers began to preach God's Word based on Scripture. Some were lay people; others were priests. Although they differed in their approach, the common thread was a desire to return to primitive Christianity and the commitment to live a simple life based on God's Word alone. Some lived barefoot or sandaled and preached to all who would listen. Their preaching was disruptive to the established order. Three similar preaching movements appeared within proximity of each other and all emphasized the importance of small groups, preaching the gospel, obedience to Scripture, and commitment to lay involvement. They were:

- The Waldensians: a Christian movement started by Peter Waldo in Lyon, France in the late 1170s. By 1215, the Waldensians were declared heretical and subject to persecution.
- The Lollards: A religious movement that existed in the mid-fourteenth century. The term Lollard refers to the followers of John Wycliffe, a prominent theologian who was dismissed from the University of Oxford in 1381 for criticism of the church. The Lollards' demands were primarily for the reform of Christianity.
- The Hussites: A Christian movement that followed the teachings of Czech reformer Jan Hus (c. 1369–1415), who became one of the forerunners of the Protestant Reformation. After Hus was put to death for alleged heresy on July 6, 1415, the Hussites continued to promote church reformation.

The following table gives an overview of the teaching of these movements:[2]

WALDENSIANS 1175	LOLLARDS 1375	HUSSITES 1400
-Conformity to the New Testament -Commitment to the vernacular -The church of Rome was corrupt -The pope was not the head of the church -Masses and prayers for the dead were without warrant -Women could minister -Sacraments administered by unworthy priests were invalid -Laymen could administer the Eucharist -Developed their own training of lay clergy	-Popes can err and a worldly pope is a heretic -The true church is made up of those elected by God; No visible church can control entrance or exclude membership -Popes nor bishops can know who the members of the true church are -Salvation does not depend upon connection with the church -Every elected person is a priest -Condemned the cult of the saints, relics, pilgrimages -Attacked transubstantiation -Layman might officiate in the Eucharist -Repudiated indulgences -Repudiated masses for the dead -Translated the Bible from the Vulgate into the vernacular	-Denounced evils of the church -Christ and not Peter was the foundation of the church -Many popes were heretics and could err -Desired moral reform rather than ecclesiastical revolution -Laity could partake in the cup of communion -The Bible was the ultimate authority

These three movements led to the Protestant Reformation, which embodied the commitment and obedience to God's Word alone. Although the Catholic Church was somewhat

2. Latourette, pp. 451-453; 662-669.

successful in quelling the voices of these pre-reformation prophets, they planted the ideological seeds that motivated and inspired those who followed.

WALDENSIANS

We already met Peter Waldo in the introduction. Waldo persuaded a sympathetic priest to translate large sections of the New Testament from Latin into the regional language, which fueled his preaching. He soon had the Gospels memorized. He then wandered throughout Lyon, France, preaching the message of Christ to anyone who would listen. A number of young men, impressed by his intelligence and sincerity, followed him in giving away their possessions and finding a new joy and freedom in simple living.

Even though he never received official permission to preach the gospel, he organized a band of followers in the city of Lyon, who became known as "the poor men of Lyon." Like Waldo, they were devoted to God's Word, poverty, and preaching the gospel. Waldo and his followers scrutinized the Bible, finding their authority to preach in God's Word, but they also discovered how the Bible contradicted the papacy in many other aspects. They realized that the Catholic Church was mistaken, not only in claiming the right to restrict their preaching, but also in the role of priests as mediators between God and human beings, noting Matthew 23:8, "All of you are brethren."

They also questioned the justification and extent of papal authority, and the interpretation of a number of biblical passages. Giorgio Tour writes, "Their calling was to be present in the churches, public squares and homes where their message could be heard. They were and wished to remain citizens of Lyon, one of the great cities of western Europe."[3]

By the early 1180s Waldo and his followers were ex-communicated and forced out of Lyon.[4] Their rejection by the Catholic Church radicalized the movement. They became anti-Catholic, rejecting the authority of the clergy, declaring any oath to be a sin, claiming anyone could preach, that the Bible alone was all that was needed for salvation, and rejecting the concept of purgatory, along with the adoration of relics and icons. Soon the movement primarily moved from house-to-house. Their house-based movement strengthened their followers and furthered their message.[5] Rad Zdero writes,

> They expanded their work all over Europe, so much so that it was believed by the canon of Notre Dame that a third of all Christendom had attended the Waldensian meetings. Their gatherings usually occurred outdoors after nightfall under the direction of an itinerant brother. After an opening prayer and sermon, they went back into their homes for supper meetings to pray, discuss, and eat the Lord's Supper.[6]

Giorgio Tour writes, "The terror of the Inquisition made public preaching, such as the earliest Waldensians had engaged in,

---

3. Giorgio Tour, *You are My Witnesses: The Waldensians across 800 Years* (Torino, Italy: Claudiana, 1989), p. 16.

4. Ibid., p. 16. Waldensians were declared schismatics by Pope Lucius III in 1184 and heretics in 1215 by the Fourth Lateran Council.

5. Latourette, p. 453.

6. Rad Zdero, *The Global House Church Movement* (Pasadena, CA: William Carey Library, 2004), p. 63.

impossible."[7] Even though they could no longer preach in the open-air, they continued to minister from house-to-house.

Waldo and his followers developed a system whereby they would go into a town and meet secretly with small groups of Waldensians. They ministered to one another in the home groups, provided hospitality to the traveling preachers, and made plans for the house-to-house ministry to continue. They would often meet in poor outlying areas, which they called *scholas* or schools. One inquisitor wrote down the confession of a Waldensian he was about to torture, who said, "In our home, women teach as well as men, and one who has been a student for a week teaches another."[8]

In these house meetings, they would gather together for a meal, pray together, and then participate in the Lord's Supper. After the meal, all would stand, join hands and lift their eyes as the leader repeated the verse from Revelation chapter seven, "Blessings, and glory, and wisdom, and thanksgiving, and honor, and might be unto our God forever and ever."[9] They worshipped as a community and read Scripture together. Describing a Waldensian home meeting, Alan Kreider writes:

> These Waldensian cells, meeting generally at night, in houses and barns, were marked by intense activity. Those present were laypeople, often "persons of basest occupations" such as tailors, shoemakers and smiths. Women were there in disproportionate strength. Largely excluded from using their gifts in the church, they were finding among the "heretics" liberty

7. Tour, p. 41.

8. Tour, p. 41.

9. Ibid., p. 41.

> to teach and preach. Everyone participated: "Old and young, men and women, by day and by night, they do not stop their learning and teaching others." Illiterates were learning to read: "Learn but one word a day," they admonished each other, "and after a year you will know three hundred, and then you will progress." The Bible was memorized and recited. In Austria one critic found an "unlearned rustic who could recite the Book of Job word for word, and many others who know the entire New Testament perfectly." After recitations, the Bible would be commented upon and applied.[10]

In 1211 more than eighty were burned as heretics at Strasbourg and centuries of severe persecution followed.[11]
Many look at the Waldensians as early Protestants because they proclaimed the Bible as the sole rule of life and faith. They rejected papal authority, indulgences, purgatory, and the doctrine of transubstantiation. Tour writes, "The problem that the Poor [Waldensians] created for the Church did not lie in their practice of the Christian life but in their commitment to preaching and to authentic Christian community."[12]

J. A. Wylie, who wrote a book on the Waldensians, says,

> The church of the Reformation was in the loins of the Waldensian Church ages before the birth of Luther . . . the Waldensians sowed the seeds of that great spiritual

---

10. Alan Kreider, "Protest And Renewal: Reformers before the Reformation" *Christian History Institute*, Vol. 9, Worcester, PA: Christian History Institute, 1986), p. 1.

11. *Martyrs' Mirror Book 1*, page 339: Burning of about 80 Waldensians, Strasbourg, 1215 (Eeghen 700).

12. Tour, p. 15.

> revival which, beginning in the days of Wycliffe, and advancing in the times of Luther and Calvin, awaits its full consummation in the ages to come.[13]

About four centuries later, the surviving Waldensians eventually accepted the Reformation doctrines. They agreed with the teachings and doctrine of John Calvin, who established systematic theology in Geneva, which was about seventy miles away from Lyon. While many Waldensian groups were absorbed into other Protestant Christian denominations, active congregations remain in Europe, South America, and North America under the label of the Waldensian Evangelical Church. Organizations such as the American Waldensian Society exist to maintain the history of this movement.

LOLLARDS

The exact origin of the term *Lollard* remains uncertain, but it is believed by many etymologists to have come from the Dutch word *lollaerd*, meaning *mumbler*. By the mid-1400s, the word had essentially become synonymous with *heretic*.

The origins of Lollardy can be traced to the writings of John Wycliffe who was a churchman, writer, and theologian, who was born sometime in the 1320s and died in 1384. Many consider Wycliffe to be the father of the English Reformation. His ideas provided a platform upon which the later reformers built. But those who followed the teaching of Wycliffe often paid a high price.

---

13. J. A. Wylie (2011-05-25) *The History of the Waldenses* (pp. 19-20). Kindle Edition.

William Sawtrey was the first Lollard to face the ultimate sacrifice. On February 12, 1401 Archbishop Thomas Arundel ordered William Sawtrey to appear at Saint Paul's Cathedral in London to give an account of his teachings. Sawtrey was an English priest who withdrew from the priesthood believing that the Bible, not church dogma, was the primary authority.

Arundel questioned William closely. Sawtrey stood firm in his conviction that it was more important to adore Christ crucified than the cross itself. Sawtrey also declared that it was a better use of time to preach to the lost than to recite religious prayers. He said that money spent on pilgrimages to save one's soul would be better spent helping the poor. However, it was his beliefs about the mass that finally got him condemned. He said that the bread of the Eucharist after consecration was indeed the bread of life, but insisted it was just bread. Roman teaching affirmed that the bread literally became Christ's flesh.

Arundel questioned him for three hours and tried to convince William to change his mind, but he refused and on February 26, 1401 William was condemned and handed over to the secular authorities to die. After his appeal was denied, he was burned to death at Smithfield in front of a crowd of spectators. He was the first "Lollard" martyr in England.

The Lollards have been called "England's first heresy." It was never an organized movement in the sense of a modern religious or secular organization. There was no "Head Lollard" or organizational hierarchy of the Lollards. Rather, the Lollards were simply people tied together by a set of beliefs. Those beliefs varied in focus and intensity from one person to the next, but some of the more common beliefs were:

- The pope had no part to play in politics
- The church was too worldly

- Monasticism had drifted from its spiritual foundation
- The Bible should be available to everyone in their own language
- True power is God's, and attempts to use power for individual gain is therefore wrong

Wycliffe taught that the church had drifted away from its spiritual foundations. He criticized papal influence in secular life and tried to make biblical teaching accessible to everyone. He thought that the Bible should be available in the language of the common people, so that everyone could read and understand it, not just those elite members of the church who were educated in Latin.

Wycliffe translated the Bible into English, which was an act of extreme courage, and one which brought him into direct conflict with the church in Rome. At the time, there were already portions of the Bible available in English, but no complete translation. "Wycliffe's Bible" as it was called, was widely distributed throughout England, and had a huge influence at the time. Predictably, it was denounced by the church as an unauthorized and inaccurate translation.

The Lollards believed the Catholic Church had been corrupted and that its claim to be the true church was not justified by Scripture or its heredity. They felt it was unbiblical for the church to say prayers for the dead and to permit chantries.[14] They believed in a lay priesthood and challenged the church's authority to invest or deny the divine authority to make a man a priest. They believed that confession to a priest was unnecessary since the priests did not have the ability to forgive sins.

---

14. A chantry was an endowment to cover expenses for the saying of masses and prayers, usually for the soul of the founder of the endowment.

They challenged the practice of clerical celibacy and believed priests should not hold government positions, which intermingled them in temporal matters.

Their belief in the priesthood of all believers stirred them to mutual accountability in home meetings—just like the early house churches. Yet their underground house meetings were also necessary because of the fierce persecution they experienced. Shannon McSheffrey examined the court evidence against the Lollards to determine their home group structure. She noticed that the Lollards tended to congregate according to homogeneous groups. She writes,

> These loose groups can be discerned from the court book evidence: groups of men, groups of married couples, and groups of women. While these categories were by no means hard and fast, it is natural that the general tendencies of social interactions in medieval society would be duplicated within Lollard communities.[15]

Robert Lutton noticed the Lollards' interconnected family relations and how the small groups were connected via the extended family. Most of those convicted of heresy were connected through a network of extended family groups. These web relationships were reminiscent of early church evangelism that spread through *oikos* or extended family evangelism. Lutton says, "Everyday or occasional relationships helped to hold the geographically disparate Kentish Lollard groups together into the more closed circles of the conventicle or household

---

15. Shannon McSheffrey, *Lollards of Coventry, 1486-1522* (Cambridge, England: Cambridge University Press, 2003), p. 37.

meetings."[16] Lutton illustrates how Lollard teachings spread through a carpenter working on someone's house and sharing his belief system.

The spread of the movement relied upon house-to-house visitation, pub evangelism, preaching in fairs and markets, conversing over meals in homes, passing out tracts, and invitations to reading circles. Lollard leaders moved from place to place in order to supervise existing groups and establish new ones. Alan Kreider writes,

> The central activity of these cells was reading the English Bible. One group in Buckinghamshire asked a boy whom they were not sure they could trust to leave them "that he should not hear and tell." Then the leader "did recite certain passages to them out of the Epistles of St Paul, and of the Gospels." These Scriptures were of course available only in manuscript, and so expensive to buy; like other English books, they were also dangerous to possess. So, although some people had good collections ("book of Luke and one of Paul. and a gloss of the Apocalypse"), many others could possess the Bible only by memorizing it. Groups of believers stayed up all night to do this. Some of them took private instruction to commit the Beatitudes to heart.[17]

The Lollard cells did not, so far as we know, administer the sacraments. They would attend their parish churches for the sacraments, even though they didn't believe that the bread

---

16. Robert Lutton, *Lollardy and Orthodox Religion in Pre-Reformation England: Reconstructing Piety* (Suffolk, England: Boydell & Brewer, 2006), p. 182.

17. Kreider, p. 1.

actually became the body of Jesus Christ. The cells didn't include membership rolls because they didn't want to draw unnecessary attention to themselves and only met in trustworthy homes or out of the way places, like barns.[18]

HUSSITES

John Hus's final sentence came on July 6, 1415. He was placed on a high stool in the middle of the church and sentenced to death. The chronicler of the event noted that they placed a hood over his head, with pictures of the devil and the word *heresiarch* (a leader of heretics), then committed his soul to the devil. Hus responded, "And I commit myself to the most gracious Lord Jesus."

In a letter written the night before his sentencing, Hus prayed that if his death would contribute anything to God's glory, then he desired to face it without fear. Hands bound behind his back, Hus was chained to the stake. Wood and hay were piled up to his chin. Rosin was sprinkled on it. He was given one last chance to recant and be set free. Bravely, he refused and said, "I shall die with joy today in the faith of the gospel which I have preached." As they lit the flames around him he sang out twice, "Christ thou Son of the Living God, have mercy upon me." He died singing and praying.

Hus was born in Husinec, Bohemia, in 1369. To escape poverty, Hus trained for the priesthood. He writes, "I had thought to become a priest quickly in order to secure a good livelihood

---

18. Stuart Murray Williams, The Lollards, www.anabaptistnetwork.com. Accessed on Wednesday, April 2, 2014.

and dress and to be held in esteem by men."[19] He eventually earned a doctorate degree, was ordained, and became the preacher at Prague's Bethlehem Chapel, which held some three thousand people. This well-known church was very influential, being located in one of Europe's most reform-minded cities.

During these years, Hus underwent a change when he discovered the Bible. Many Czech students, in fact, studied at Oxford, and carried Wycliffe's ideas back to Prague. Hus, who became Rector of the University of Prague, read Wycliffe's teachings, accepted them, and taught many of his ideas. Hus's preaching attracted a huge following, including Bohemian rulers.

He tried to reform the church by attacking moral failings of clergy, bishops, and even the papacy from his pulpit. Hus was disillusioned with the state of the church, particularly the spectacle of two, and then three rival popes at once. The archbishop of Prague tolerated Hus and even appointed him as preacher to the clergy's synod. Some of the rulers joined his cause because they were embroiled in the fight for equality with the Catholic powers of the Holy Roman Empire. The University of Prague was already split between Czechs and Germans, and Wycliffe's teachings only divided them more.

Hus began to increasingly trust the Scriptures only, "desiring to hold, believe, and assert whatever is contained in them as long as I have breath in me." A political struggle ensued, with the Germans labeling Hus and his followers as heretics. With the support of the king of Bohemia, the Czechs gained the upper hand, and the Germans were forced to flee to other

---

19. John Hus, Christian History, ChristianityHistory.net, www.christianity today.com/ch/131christians/martyrs/, p. 1. Accessed in April 2014.

universities. In 1405 Pope Innocent VII demanded that the archbishop counter Hus's heretical teachings, and the archbishop complied.

Although John Hus didn't establish a system of small groups, he forged the path through biblical preaching to what some have called the "Hussite Reformation" or "Czech Reformation."[20] These Hussites formed the *Unitas Fratrum* (Unity of Brethren) in 1457, and the church grew primarily through house-to-house ministry in its homelands of Bohemia and Moravia to a membership of two hundred thousand.[21] They created the first truly voluntary church in western history. Craig Atwood writes,

> They [Unity of Brethren] associated the state church with the emperor Constantine, who they believed brought the oppression and violence of the Roman Empire into the church. . . . The Brethren also taught that there is no true Christianity without a visible community of love. Their understanding of Christian community was inspired by the example of the early church of the apostles. [22]

The Hussites were forced to meet in underground house churches, especially during the fierce persecution of the Thirty Years War (1618-1648). These Hussites clung to their passionate desire to return to primitive Christianity. They rejected everything that had no basis in the Bible, such as the veneration

---

20. Craig D. Atwood, *The Theology of the Czech Brethren from Hus to Comenius* (University Park, PA: Penn State Press, 2009), p. 5.

21. Tarunjit Singh Butalia, Dianne p. Small, *Religion in Ohio: Profiles of Faith Communities* (Athens, OH : Ohio University Press, 2004), p. 193.

22. Atwood, p. 5.

of saints, images, fasts, superfluous holidays, the oath, intercession for the dead, auricular confession, and indulgences.

Hussite cell groups continued to meet until being relocated approximately two hundred years later to Count Zinzendorf's estate—who we will meet in a later chapter. Zinzendorf started the modern missionary movement and the Hussites, who later adopted the name *Unitas Fratrum* (United Brethren), comprised the core group that made the modern missionary movement possible.[23]

LESSONS LEARNED

- Pre-reformation movements, like the Waldensians, Lollards, and Hussites, believed in God's Word as the basis for their authority, resisted Catholic dogma, and emphasized a simple lifestyle.
- These movements emphasized the priesthood of all believers and a return to primitive Christianity, as opposed to the hierarchical leadership common in the Roman Catholic Church.
- Home groups were the natural habitat of these pre-reformation movements.
- These movements were persecuted severely by the Roman Catholic Church, who saw them as divisive and disruptive of the status quo.
- These pre-reformation movements pointed out church abuses that were not based on God's Word. They paved the way for Luther's reformation.

---

23. Accessed at http://www.cob-net.org/docs/groups.htm on Wednesday, April 2, 2014.

Chapter 5

LUTHER AND SMALL GROUPS

In the sixteenth century, the world was divided about Martin Luther. One Catholic thought Martin Luther was a "demon in the appearance of a man." Another who first questioned Luther's theology later declared, "He alone is right!" Most today would affirm he was not only right about a great deal, but he changed the course of western history for the better.

The greatest contribution of Martin Luther was the rediscovery of the truth of justification by faith alone and the authority of Scripture. He also recaptured the understanding that the church was no longer the institution defined by apostolic succession; instead it was the community of faith. Salvation came not by the sacraments but through faith in Christ. Faith no longer consisted of assenting to the church's teachings but by trusting the promises of God and the merits of Christ.

Luther was fortunate to avoid the fatal persecution of the pre-reformation groups. He enjoyed a degree of social and political support that allowed his theology to penetrate deeply into the fabric of church and society. However, Luther acknowledged his gratitude for those who paved the way and even declared himself a "Hussite," along with the apostle Paul.[1]

In fact, those living in Bohemia saw in Martin Luther a continuation of Hus's reforms. Yet, there were key differences as well. The Hussites were more concerned about sanctification, becoming the true church, and resisting the state church practice. Luther, on the other hand, highlighted the theological doctrines of grace, faith alone, the priesthood of all believers, and the authority of Scripture. Unlike the Hussites, he also secured the political protection to maintain the changes he started.

LUTHER CONSIDERS SMALL GROUPS TO PROMOTE HOLINESS

One of the key doctrines that Luther taught was the priesthood of the believer. He believed that each believer could read the Bible, understand Scripture's plain meaning, have equal access

1. Rudolf Rican, *The History of the Unity of the Brethren* (Salem, NC: The Moravian Church in America, 1992), p. 108.

to God, and be actively involved as a minister of the gospel. Initially Luther looked for ways to apply the priesthood of all believers and entertained the idea of using small groups as part of the church's reformation. However, he failed to implement use of small groups for reasons noted in the following sections: *Later Change of Mind* and *Anabaptist Storm Gathering.*

In a number of his tracts, Luther expressed his concern about the Mass and Liturgy, and even hinted at the need for house gatherings. In his preface to the *German Mass and Order of Service*, he said,

> The third kind of service should be a truly evangelical order and should not be held in a public place for all sorts of people. But those who want to be Christians in earnest and who profess the gospel with hand and mouth should sign their names and meet alone in a house somewhere to pray, to read, to baptize, to receive the sacrament, and to do other Christian works. . . . Here one could set up a brief and neat order for baptism and the sacrament and center everything on the Word, prayer and love . . .[2]

Luther saw the potential of the house church and had a vision of meeting in homes for deeper expression of faith, which was absent in the institutional church. We know from Luther's writings that he could see great possibilities for ministry in the small house churches, but he refused to go that route because of cultural ramifications.

---

2. Martin Luther, "Preface to the German Mass and Order of Service," *Luther Works*, Vol. 53, Helmut T. Lehman, ed. (Philadelphia, PA: Fortress Press, 1965), pp. 63-64.

LATER CHANGE OF MIND

Although Luther spoke of the importance of small groups, he never implemented them. The answer to why he never followed through came from a personal letter discovered in 1982. Luther wrote on April 14, 1529 to a fellow priest named Karl Weiss, saying he had "changed his mind" about the formation of small groups, stating that he no longer believed that "earnest Christians" should meet together in the home in order "to pray, to read, to baptize, to receive the sacrament, and to do other Christian works . . ."[3] Here are the reasons given in the letter for Luther's change of mind:

First, Luther thought that people would fool themselves about who is an earnest Christian. He believed that an "earnest Christian" might fall into pride and a lack of understanding of grace. He wrote, "He [Satan] would be able to get us to isolate all the strongest Christians, and keep them from the weak. Then the strong would grow proud, the weak would give up, and all would go to hell in a handbasket."[4]

Second, Luther believed ". . . that such self-styled 'earnest Christians' will start to think of themselves as the one, pure church."[5] Luther warned, "If we allow small groups of Christians to separate from the rest, to read the Word, to baptize, and

---

3. Charles E. White, ed. "Concerning Earnest Christians: A Newly Discovered Letter of Martin Luther" *Currents in Theology and Mission*, 1983, 10 (5): p. 274.

4. Ibid., p. 278.

5. Ibid., p. 275.

to receive sacraments, we will have established a new church."[6] From this quote we can clearly see that Luther wanted everyone in Germany to come under the one church—under the one umbrella. Luther feared the potential divisiveness of small groups. He wrote,

> All the elements [of the true church] would be there in these small groups and, as sure as Satan seeks to destroy our souls, some Pharisaical spirit will conclude that his little group is the church, and that everyone outside is damned. Indeed, it has already happened, if I am to believe the rumor I hear. Certain false brethren rebaptize themselves and then sneak away from God's church to meet with other misled fools in various holes and corners. They claim that they are the only true Christians, and teach that they must separate from all iniquity.[7]

Luther did not believe that it was scriptural to separate from the church to set up a pure group of earnest Christians. In fact, by 1529 Luther had come to the conclusion that there was no scriptural warrant for such small groups. Rather, he quotes passages to indicate that the true church always maintained a mixture of both the pure and the impure.[8]

ANABAPTIST STORM GATHERING

When Luther first wrote about earnest Christians meeting together in 1526, the Anabaptist movement was just getting

6. Ibid.

7. Ibid., p. 275.

8. Ibid., pp. 276-277.

under way. However, it was in February, 1527 that the articles of faith for the Anabaptist movement were written and officially declared. Just three months after the signing of those documents, Michael Slater, one of the key Anabaptist authors, was burned at the stake.[9] Although Luther felt that small groups would be helpful for the church (as seen in his 1526 preface), his fear of the Anabaptist movement and the division it could cause, changed his thinking (as seen the 1529 letter).

D. M. Lloyd-Jones points out that Luther became depressed as the reformation continued, knowing that many felt like he had not taken it far enough. Lloyd-Jones writes,

> Another thing that greatly aggravated this feeling [of depression] which developed in him was the phenomenon of Anabaptist [teaching] . . . He had to admit that there was a quality of life in their churches which was absent in the churches to which he belonged. So he reacts in two ways to them; he has got to discipline his people against them, and yet he wishes to have in his church the kind of thing that was working so well in their churches. The result of all this was that he felt that the only thing to do was . . . to gather together the people who are truly Christian into a kind of inner church.[10]

---

9. Latourette, p. 782.

10. D. M. Lloyd Jones, "Ecclesiola in Ecclesia," Approaches to the Reformation of the Church, (Papers from the Puritan and Reformed Studies Conference), 1965, pp. 60-61, as quoted in Bill Beckham, *The Second Reformation* (Houston, TX: Touch Publications, 1995), p. 116.

Luther, along with Zwingli and the other reformers, could not fully encourage others to practice the priesthood of all believers because they needed the protection of the government and the stability of the entire state to embrace their reforms. The ability to sustain their movement against the Roman Catholic authorities required that everyone in the state become followers of Luther's revolutionary cause. The priesthood of all believers had little practical application in the state-run church. We know that Luther felt responsible for the revolution he was leading, since the rulers had already stepped out of their normal boundaries to support and protect Luther. Luther owed those rulers his allegiance.

But suddenly, this growing Anabaptist movement was tearing away the very fabric of the culture and possibly costing Luther the revolution. In reality, the Anabaptists were simply taking Luther's doctrine to its logical conclusion. They were following Scripture, which taught the priesthood of all believers, the early church house gatherings, and a more simple hierarchy.

Meeting in home groups was Luther's unwritten thesis which he believed, but failed to implement because of a spirit of caution, political considerations, and fear of losing the movement to the Anabaptists.

LESSONS LEARNED

- Martin Luther displayed a rare combination of intellectual brilliance matched with incredible courage and commitment to stand on his convictions.
- God used Martin Luther to start a new type of church based on God's Word, rather than church tradition.

- Although Luther transformed theology, he never implemented the priesthood of all believers through small groups. He failed to significantly change the ecclesiastical structure, baptizing all infants into the state church.
- Luther overreacted to potential dangers of small groups in the Anabaptist movement and instead of warning against potential dangers and moving to middle ground, he ended up rejecting the small group emphasis entirely.

Chapter 6

MARTIN BUCER AND SMALL GROUPS

Writing in 1539, John Calvin described Martin Bucer as a man "who on account of his profound scholarship, his bounteous knowledge about a wide range of subjects, his keen mind, his wide reading, and many other different virtues, remains unsurpassed today by anyone, can be compared with only a few, and excels the vast majority."[1] Calvin wrote these words during his three year stay in Strasbourg (1538–1541), where Bucer was a prominent reformer.

In 1538, Bucer invited John Calvin to lead a French refugee congregation in Strasbourg. Bucer and Calvin had much in common theologically and maintained a long friendship. The extent to which Bucer influenced Calvin is an open question among modern scholars, but many of the reforms that Calvin later implemented in Geneva were originally developed in Strasbourg. After his arrival in the city, Calvin lived for a time in Bucer's house before moving into a house with a backyard that adjoined Bucer's backyard. During this time the two reformers became close, and Bucer greatly influenced his younger colleague. Yet in spite of the close connection between Bucer and Calvin, Bucer remains relatively unknown by many Reformed Christians.

STRASBOURG: A HOTBED OF THE REFORMATION

Bucer converted to Protestant Christianity in 1521 after reading the works of Luther. Excommunicated by the Roman Catholic Church in 1522, he moved to Strasbourg where he became a Protestant leader. Strasbourg, France in the 1500s was strongly anti-clerical. The people could see how clergymen and monks lived free of the constraints and obligations of civic laws and didn't have to earn their own living, like everyone else. Clerics led a life of luxury and comfort, paying no taxes other than

---

1. As quoted by Keith Anderson, blog on *Martin Bucer: A Reformer and His Times* (Ligonier Ministries, August 24, 2010). Accessed at http://www.ligonier.org/blog/martin-bucer-reformer-and-his-times.

a symbolic fee for the city's protection.[2] As the reformation rolled along and the people were able to read their Bibles, they began to question the role and practices of the clergy.

Government officials in Strasbourg translated some sixteen publications of Martin Luther, and the people gladly followed Luther's teachings.[3] Bucer drew heavily from Luther's theology but emphasized more of a practical, pastoral theology, as opposed to Luther's theological leanings. Bucer was not so concerned about staking a unique doctrinal claim among the reformers. Rather, he is chiefly remembered for his promotion of doctrinal unity and his lifelong struggle to create an inclusive church, rather than winning doctrinal arguments. He envisioned the ideal society to be one that was led by an enlightened, God-centered government with all the people united under Christian fellowship.

ECCLESIOLOGICAL REFORM THROUGH SMALL GROUPS

Bucer became increasingly drawn to the model of the primitive church which emphasized both large and small groups. He felt that small groups would make the church at Strasbourg ". . . more faithful to the primitive and ancient churches."[4] D. F. Wright comments,

2. Martin Greschat, *Martin Bucer: A Reformer and His Times* (Louisville, Kentucky: Westminster John Knox Press, 2004), p. 50.

3. Ibid., p. 54.

4. D.F. Wright, *Martin Bucer: Reforming Church and Community* (Cambridge, MA: Cambridge University Press, 1994), p. 142.

> In specifying how the small communities would function, the Reformer sought ever closer conformity to the pattern of the organization and life of the apostolic communities, as described in the New Testament Acts and Epistles. . . . Not only confession of the same doctrine, but also demonstration of the same practice must attest to this apostolic faithfulness—hence, for example, the insistence on the sharing of goods on the model of the communities described in Acts 2 and 4.[5]

He believed that the primitive church should be the normative model, and he often lamented the deficiencies of the Strasbourg church when compared with the early church communities.[6] Although he believed strongly in justification by faith, he also knew that justification needed to be lived out through sanctification, and he didn't want one to be excluded from the other. Small groups were a practical way to work out sanctification.

When he implemented his small group model, he only allowed serious believers to join. In fact a potential member had to be interviewed by the pastor and the elders of that particular group. The interview dealt with members' beliefs concerning doctrine, the sacraments, Christian behavior, and repentance. In early 1547 he developed his small group strategy, which included:

- Those who wanted a deeper commitment were invited to join a small group community.
- A leadership team was developed to guide the groups.
- The purpose was to help members grow in holiness, confess sin, and be held accountable to each other.

---

5. Ibid., pp. 142-143.

6. Ibid., pp. 136,137.

- The goal was to restore primitive Christianity in the church.
- The groups were connected to each other.
- The leaders met each week.
- All the groups would come together for a larger meeting once every two months.

IMPLEMENTATION OF GROUPS IN THE FACE OF CRITICISM

Bucer faced continual pressure and criticism for his small group model. As the leading reformer of Strasbourg, he found himself at the heart of the Anabaptist debate.[7] On one hand, there were many Anabaptists living in Strasbourg who promoted a separate, voluntary church. Yet, Bucer was heavily influenced by Luther's larger reform in Germany and had to walk a fine line because he also depended on the protection of the political elite.

In the mid-1540s, Anabaptism rapidly increased in numbers and influence, and Anabaptist small groups met all around Strasbourg. In light of this, it was risky for Bucer to advocate further reform and suggest the possibility of forming small groups for discipleship and spiritual growth. Wright notes,

> The more Bucer pressed the magistracy to devote all its energies to the introduction of a "true" ecclesiastical discipline, the more the Strasbourg church seemed doomed to degeneration and criticism. Nasty tongues spread scandal about the town and its Reformers . . .[8]

7. Wright, p. 134.

8. Ibid., p. 135.

He understood the strong points in the Anabaptist movement, but he had to make sure there was enough support for his reforms to succeed. He had to manage the reformation in Strasbourg, make sure the state church was following him, and reform the church in the process. Wright says,

> The creation of groups and other gatherings which . . . could easily be likened to the separatist ventures of the Anabaptists and other sectarians, exposed him to insidious criticism charging him with a share of responsibility for the fragmentation of Strasbourg's church community.[9]

Yet, in spite of all of the criticism, Bucer was compelled to press ahead. He realized that a house church structure was not an Anabaptist phenomenon but rather a New Testament imperative. He understood that primitive Christianity challenged the reformation to take steps toward change.

THE LARGE AND SMALL GATHERING

For Bucer, it was not a matter of deciding to support the inclusive state church or the church gathered in homes. Rather, he felt the need for both. Wright concludes, "This motif of twofold ecclesiology, at once both majority-based and confessing, played an important role in the slow maturation of his plans for small communities."[10] He felt that he would have actually been "unfaithful" to Scripture if he did not promote the gathering of believers in small groups. He was the first true forerunner of cell-based ministry because he desired to connect the gathered church with the scattered church.

---

9. Ibid., p. 140.

10. Wright, p. 134.

Bucer explained to his critics that instead of creating divisiveness, the small groups aimed specifically at promoting unity among the believers. The Sunday morning worship service would bring them all together. In fact, Bucer felt that the communion table on Sunday morning was the perfect time for the "true" Christian community to meet.

The Anabaptists wanting to separate from the gathered church by promoting independent meetings. Yet Bucer felt the need to maintain the gathered church but also to promote small groups of Christians, much like the early church.[11] Peter Burton writes,

> His position, however, was not that of the Anabaptists, who held to the notion of the believer's church. It was, in essence, a kind of synthesis between two different concepts of church, namely the majority church and the confession church; it seems he wanted both combined."[12]

As the resistance to his ideas became stronger, Bucer became increasingly despondent.

SHORT-LIVED REFORMS

The criticisms intensified as many felt that Bucer was promoting two classes of Christians: those who were in the small groups and those who were just part of the normal church. The state felt that he was giving too much power to the lay people. He yielded to their criticism and stopped the groups in

---

11. Peter Bunton, *Cell Groups and House Churches* (Ephrata, PA: House to House Publications, 2001), p. 11.

12. Ibid., p. 11.

1548, after having implemented them for only about 1.5 years.[13] Later Bucer moved to England and taught at Cambridge. Perhaps his greatest contribution was the writings he left behind, which later had a powerful influence on Spener and then later Wesley. After his death, his writings continued to be translated, reprinted, and disseminated throughout Europe.

LESSONS LEARNED

- Although fully committed to reformation teachings, Bucer also wanted to practice those teachings through the implementation of small groups.
- He continued to emphasize small groups in the face of major criticisms because he believed in the scriptural basis for house-to-house ministry as coming from Acts and the early church.
- Bucer's reforms through small groups were short lived. We don't hear much about his small group reforms because he was not able to stay with it long enough to maintain the changes.
- The philosophy and lifestyle of small group ministry requires a long period of transitional change to become part of the church and culture. There is often resistance in the process, as was the case with Martin Bucer's small group reforms.

13. Ibid., pp. 13-14.

Chapter 7

THE ANABAPTISTS

Dirk Willems of Holland was re-baptized when he became a believer, rejecting the infant baptism practiced at that time. This action, plus his continued devotion to his new faith, led to his arrest and martyrdom. An officer came to arrest him at the village of Asperen. Running for his life, Dirk came to a frozen pond. After making his way across in great peril, he realized that his pursuer had fallen through the ice, and into the freezing water.

Turning back to save the drowning officer, Dirk dragged him safely to shore. The man wanted to release Dirk, but a chief magistrate, having appeared on the scene, reminded him that he was under oath to deliver criminals to justice. Dirk was bound off to prison, interrogated, and tortured in an unsuccessful effort to make him renounce his faith.

He was tried and found guilty of having been re-baptized, of holding secret meetings in his home, and of allowing baptism there—all of which he freely confessed. "Persisting obstinately in his opinion," Dirk was burned at the stake near his hometown on May 16, 1569—enduring it with great steadfastness.

ADULT BAPTISM

The Anabaptists believed in the reformation teachings of Zwingli, Luther, and Calvin. They agreed with the biblical doctrines of justification by faith and that the Bible was the sole basis for authority in the Christian life. Yet, both Protestants and Catholics rejected the Anabaptists, and even hunted them down. The Anabaptist movement's most distinctive, and hated tenet was adult baptism, which was a crime punishable by death under the legal codes of the time.

Living in an age of religious pluralism, we wonder why people in the sixteenth century would be tortured or drowned over baptism. The fierce resistance to this practice had more to do with culture than Christianity. In other words, to be baptized was a civil issue, and those who refused to be baptized as an infant tore at the seams of a Christian society. When Luther, Zwingli, and others led their movements away from Catholicism, many practices were changed. But infant baptism, the accepted baptismal mode for most of Christian history, was not. Baptizing only adults tore at the heart of both church and state.

Many prefer the name *radical reformation* when referring to the Anabaptist movement. In fact, those within the movement rejected the label *Anabaptist,* which literally means *rebaptizer.* They repudiated their own baptism as infants as a blasphemous formality. They considered the public confession of sin and faith, sealed by adult baptism, to be the only proper baptism. They held that infants are not punishable for sin until they become aware of good and evil and can exercise their own free will, repent, and accept baptism.

Although Felix Manz was the first Anabaptist martyr put to death for conducting illegal baptisms, many more martyrs followed. Latham notes, "Their re-baptism was the action of disobedience which placed them in direct opposition to the secular and religious authorities."[1] And the state church reacted by persecuting them severely. Latourette says, "Late in the 1520s and early in the 1530s hundreds of Anabaptists were killed, some by drowning, some by beheading, and others by burning."[2]

REFORMING THE CHURCH

The Anabaptists believed that the church, the community of those who have made a public commitment of faith, should be separated from the state, which they believed existed only for the punishment of sinners. They were determined to restore the institutions and spirit of the primitive church and identified their sufferings with the early martyrs. Confident that they were living at the end of time, they expected the imminent return of Jesus Christ.

---

1. Jane Holly Latham, "In Search of the True Church: An Examination of the Significance of Small Groups within Early Anabaptism and Pietism" (M.A. thesis, Acadia University, 1992), p. 24.

2. Latourette, p. 782.

The seriousness of their Christianity and their commitment to discipleship can be seen by the fact that they would often meet together four or five times per week.[3] Writing about their commitment, Jane Holly Latham says,

> When someone followed the Anabaptist doctrine, he/she was expected to separate him/herself from the world and follow a new way of life. The new way of life excluded them from most of their community's social functions.[4]

The Anabaptists clung to the priesthood of all believers. They resisted the tendency of the magisterial church to dictate who should lead the church. John D. Roth says,

> In contrast to the social and class distinctions that persisted in the magisterial churches, Anabaptists insisted that within the gathered community no one ought to lord over anyone else. Upon baptism, each male promised to accept the responsibilities of leadership but the final selection of leaders was left to the providence of God.[5]

The radical brethren longed to move closer to New Testament Christianity and to emphasize the priesthood of each believer.

---

3. Tan, p. 46.

4. Latham, p. 12.

5. John D. Roth, "Pietism and the Anabaptist," *The Dilemma of Anabaptist Piety*, chapter 1, Stephen L. Longenecker, ed. (Bridgewater, VA: Penobscot Press, 1997), p. 26.

LAY-LED CELLS

In 1522, those with Anabaptist tendencies gathered in homes for small, private meetings. These meetings expanded into a wave of lay reading groups, which met mainly in Zurich and the surrounding area. They met together to strengthen their faith and grow in biblical knowledge. At one time even Zwingli, the Zurich reformer, attended and promoted these small groups, commenting that as a result of these meetings the lay people were better acquainted with the Scriptures than some priests.[6]

Their meetings were clear examples of lay-led cell group gatherings. They saw themselves as Christ's church meeting in homes. Latham comments,

> The Brethren came together because they felt that the limits of the Zwinglian reforms were suppressing the truth. Meeting together in private, the Brethren hoped to discover the truth and obtain scriptural guidance for church reforms, which they believed were being suppressed by Zwingli and the Town Council.[7]

They desired to return to primitive Christianity and meeting in small groups gave them ample opportunity to practice the priesthood of all believers. However, in 1523, Anabaptists Conrad Grebel and Simon Stumpf proposed that the church should be separated from the rest of society in order to establish a church consisting solely of true Christians. This idea took their reforms one step further and caused Zwingli, the

6. Latham, p. 15.

7. Ibid., p. 17.

official reform leader in Zurich, to strongly disagree and even oppose the Anabaptists.[8]

CIRCUMSTANTIAL NECESSITY FOR SMALL GROUPS

Although small groups played a vital part of the Anabaptist movement throughout the sixteenth century, it's hard to say whether or not the Anabaptists met in homes due to their theological convictions or because of circumstantial necessity. Latham concludes her dissertation on the Anabaptist movement by saying,

> As well as being used as an effective means of evangelism and cultivation of the Anabaptist faith, the small group was also employed out of necessity. Anabaptists met in small groups because all Anabaptist activity was illegal. The Anabaptist concept of the church as a gathered community combined together to produce the small group meeting as the movement's main mode of existence.[9]

Would the Anabaptists have constructed their own buildings if they could have done so? Or was their small group meetings a matter of choice? According to Jim and Carol Plueddemann, even after the Anabaptist persecution waned, they still preferred to meet in homes because they felt it was closer to the practice of the early church.[10] They eventually came to believe that they

---

8. Ibid., p. 17.

9. Latham, pp. 110-111.

10. Jim and Carol Plueddemann, *Pilgrims in Progress* (Wheaton, IL: Harold Shaw Publishers, 1990), pp. 6-7.

were fulfilling the functions of the true church (as opposed to the state church) and that their home groups helped emphasize the church as a group of believing, baptized adults.

LESSONS LEARNED

- The Anabaptists, unlike many of the earlier reformers, believed that only baptized adults should gather as the church.
- They rejected the ecclesiastical institutions that baptized infants, seeing this as subversive to true Christianity.
- They were willing to resist the state church and live out the reforms of Luther and the other reformers, although they were severely persecuted for it.
- The Anabaptist movement can best be compared with the early house church movement that freely met together as committed believers.
- While many reformers only talked about the reformation of the church and the priesthood of all believers, the Anabaptists paid for this reform with their own lives.

Chapter 8

PURITAN CONVENTICLES

When people think of the early English Puritans, they often imagine sour legalists who tried to prevent people from doing what they desired to do. This view comes from later American history and people such as Nathaniel Hawthorne, who were glad to be living under liberal Unitarianism in New England and regarded the old Puritanism of their forefathers as a repressive, false religion.

Yet the original Puritans were not from New England but from Great Britain and the word Puritan described those in England who believed that the Reformation had not truly transformed the English state church. Only later would many of the English Puritans migrate to America to start a new life. Yet, the original Puritans were dissatisfied with the brand of Protestantism called Anglicanism. They wanted to purify the Anglican Church.

The Puritans were the English equivalent of the continental reformers. C. S. Lewis said, "We must picture these Puritans as the very opposite of those who bear that name today: as young, fierce, progressive intellectuals, very fashionable and up-to-date. They were not teetotalers; bishops, not beer, were their special aversion. . . ."[1] These Puritans were the "young bucks" who wanted to go all the way with God and the Bible. They were excited about biblical truth and couldn't imagine why anybody would want to hide it under superstition and human traditions. They felt that the English Reformation had not extended far enough, and that the Church of England was tolerant of practices which they associated with the Catholic Church.

The Puritans formed and joined forces with various religious groups advocating greater "purity" of worship and doctrine, as well as personal and group piety. Those who remained within the Church of England were known as "non-separating Puritans." Those who felt that the Church of England was so corrupt that true Christians should separate from it altogether were known as "separating Puritans" or simply "Separatists." "Puritan," in the wider sense, includes both groups.

As Puritans looked at the Church of England's spirituality and doctrine in the sixteenth and seventeenth centuries, they

---

1. As quoted by Mark S. Ritchie, "The Protestant Reformation" (The Story of the Church - Part 4, Topic 7), www.ritchies.net. Accessed in April 2014.

saw wickedness and religiosity. Although the theology was reformed and most believed in the doctrines of Calvin, it was clear to many believers that there was much, much more to the Christian life than what they were seeing.[2] So how did the Puritans resist the status quo? Many separated. Alan Simpson writes,

> Carried to its fullest extent, it meant separation: the duty to separate from the polluted mass of mankind. So little groups of saints peeled off from the national church under the leadership of a minister to meet surreptitiously in each other's houses, to migrate to the Netherlands if England is made too uncomfortable for them, and to experience, wherever they go, the perplexities as well as the privileges of their strange adventure.[3]

This separation or holiness took place over a period of a century, followed by fifty years of immigration. Eventually the English Puritans spread to places like New England and eventually the rest of America.

WHAT DID THEY BELIEVE?

The Puritans in England adopted a Reformed theology and, in that sense, were Calvinists. Describing Puritan theology, Peter Lewis writes, "Vastly Calvinistic in their theological tradition, they treasured a high conception of the sovereignty of God in providence and grace, and reflected this in the tranquility

---

2. Alan Simpson, *Puritanism in Old and New England* (Chicago, IL: The University of Chicago Press, 1955), p. 10.

3. Simpson, p. 14.

with which they were able to carry themselves in the stormiest experiences."[4]

The Puritans also held a very high view of the church. They desired to return to New Testament Christianity and weren't going to allow kings and monarchs to dictate how the church was supposed to function.[5] Even though Puritans in England were blocked from changing the established Anglican Church from within, their views were transported by emigration to the Netherlands, New England, Ireland, and Wales. Around 1630, many Puritans left for New England to start the Massachusetts Bay Colony and other settlements. The large-scale Puritan emigration to New England ceased by 1641, with around twenty-one thousand having moved across the Atlantic. This English-speaking Puritan population in America produced more than sixteen million descendants.

Migration brought out many differences in Puritan thought and lifestyle. As soon as Puritans reached American shores, their views on church governance diverged from those of Puritans remaining in the British Isles, who faced different issues. Alexis de Tocqueville suggested in *Democracy in America* that Puritanism was the very thing that provided a firm foundation for American democracy. As Sheldon Wolin puts it, "Tocqueville was aware of the harshness and bigotry of the early colonists." On the other hand, he saw them as "archaic survivals, not only in their piety and discipline but in their democratic practices."[6]

---

4. Peter Lewis, *The Genius of Puritanism* (Haywards Heath Sussex, Great Britain: Carey Publications, 1975), p. 12.

5. Ibid., p. 15.

6. Taken from the article, "Puritan," in Wikipedia at http://en.wikipedia.org/wiki/Puritan. Accessed on Wednesday, December 11, 2013.

CONVENTICLES

Conventicles, or small group gatherings, were one of the key practices by which the Puritans matured as believers. The word *conventicle* refers to an unlawful or secret religious gathering. During the period of 1570-1620 the term *prophecy meetings* was also used. These meetings were based on 1 Corinthians 14, which speaks about prophesy in the early house churches. During these meetings, the believers emphasized prayer, Scripture reading, Bible memorization, and application of the sermon to the daily lives of those present.

Conventicles multiplied throughout England to meet the need of community and spiritual growth. Francis Couvares writes, "English Puritans—including those who later emigrated to the New World—had not tempered their intellectual and social bonds at any single ideological forge but over the spiritual flames of countless private emotional meetings or 'conventicles' throughout England."[7] They grew as they discussed Scripture together and tried to apply it to their daily lives.

The English crown did their best to snuff out those flames. Queen Elizabeth viewed the group meetings as seditious. She felt that the preaching of a sermon once per month was sufficient. When Archbishop Edmund Grindal protested the suppression of prophesying and refused compliance with the royal command, Elizabeth stripped him of all his duties and powers as an officer of the Crown and sequestered him in his palace under house arrest until his death. Royal commissioners

7. Francis Couvares, *Interpretations of American History Vol. I: Patterns and Perspectives* (New York: Simon and Schuster, 2000), p. 54.

were appointed to exercise his duties and powers as a minister of the state. The official law stated:

> NO Minister shall preach, or administer the holy Communion, in any private house, except it be in times of necessity, when any being either so impotent as he cannot go to the church, or very dangerously sick, are desirous to be partakers of that holy Sacrament, under pain of suspension for the first offence, and excommunication for the second (Canon 71)

Canon 72 clarifies even further, stating that "NO Minister or Ministers shall, without the licence and direction of the Bishop of the diocese first obtained and had under his hand and seal, appoint or keep any solemn Fasts, either publickly [original spelling] or in any private houses."[8]

GROWING TOGETHER

Many conventicles were simply called *fellowship meetings*. The Puritans believed that the gospel transformation wasn't complete until a person was committed to fellowship with other believers. The Puritans grew in their experiential knowledge of the Trinity, as they communed with one another in the conventicles. Even though the Puritans believed in individual passion and zeal, they rejected religious individualism, believing that God called believers into a life of community.

Spiritual fellowship was supposed to happen at church, at home, and among friends. Richard Sibbes, an early Puritan wrote,

---

8. Robin G. Jordan, "The History of Home Fellowships," (Anglicans Ablaze website, www.anglicansablaze.blogspot.com). Accessed on Thursday, April 3, 2014.

"The church is like a hospital—people need one another—a common hospital where all are in some measure sick, thus we should have ground of exercising mutually the spirit of wisdom and of meekness."[9] Sibbes goes on to say, "There is such a thing as sweet communion of saints whereby we encourage and comfort one another in the ways of holiness and draw and allure others to the best things."[10]

As the church met in conventicles, Puritans believed that they would grow more and more mature in understanding the Scriptures, and become richer in experimental knowledge of the work of the Triune God. And everyone participated—not just the men. Walter E. Van Beek notes,

> In the conventicles, women are not simply passive listeners, they participate in the discussions in exactly the same way as men. The term 'Mothers in Israel' expresses the deep respect for converted women and women participate on a par with men. Of course, women cannot lead congregations as ministers or elders.[11]

Most who participated in conventicles continued as part of the Anglican state church. They simply wanted more spiritual food and edification for their souls than the state church offered. Conventicles were, according to Voetius, necessary as

---

9. As quoted in Hans Molenaar, "The Historical Development of Conventicles," Thesis at Puritan Reformed Theological Seminary (Grand Rapids, MI: 2005), p. 17.

10. Ibid., p. 17.

11. Walter E. Van Beek, *The Quest for Purity: Dynamics of Puritan Movements* (New York : Mouton de Gruyter, 1988) p. 100.

a powerful way to equip God's people and to grow in grace, or, as he wrote, "to grow in piety." A Puritan conventicle included:

- Prayer, the singing of psalms and hymns (James 5:13; Colossians 3:16; Ephesians 5:19)
- Reading of Scripture
- Discussion of recent sermons (Matthew 13:5 and Mark 4:10)
- Discussion of what God was showing them through reading and listening to God
- Speaking about the workings of the sovereignty of God
- Teaching and learning the ways of the Lord seen in the life of his people

In the Puritan way of thinking, it was critical that each person had the phrase "Holiness to the Lord" figuratively written on his or her forehead. Men and women were called to flee sin and to walk in God's ways. God's way to walk in holiness was faithfully attending the worship service, prioritizing the family, and worshipping in groups.[12] The influence of Puritan conventicles is seen in this quote by Francis Couvares,

> From these private meetings [conventicles], which perhaps more than any institution or idea provided Puritans with a group identity, sprang not only the likes of John Winthrop, Thomas Hooker, Thomas Shepard, and others who became staunch supporters of non-separating congregationalism, but also those individuals who by the mid-1640s had helped to generate a myriad of radical Puritan sects that threatened to

12. Molenaar, p. 46.

fulfill the prophecy of Acts 17:6 and turn the known world upside down.[13]

The holding of conventicles helped revive the church of Jesus Christ. J. Edwin Orr writes, "Just before the fifteenth century something started to change the church. It resulted in a progression of spiritual awakenings in which small groups either spearheaded, became strong catalysts of, or followed as nurturing environments to revivals."[14] This awakening that J. Edwin Orr talked about back then is the same direction God is taking his church today. Whenever there has been a revival, small groups have played a vital function.

LESSONS LEARNED

- The English Puritans, like many who went before them, felt the church was too traditional and not living according to the New Testament pattern. God used the Puritan conventicles to spiritually awaken the church.
- The Puritans viewed the primitive church and their house-to-house ministry as the way to create a more biblical, pure church.
- The English conventicles were one of the main ways by which the English Puritans grew in community and holiness.
- As Puritans migrated to North America and other parts of Europe, they adapted, but never lost, the zeal to practice biblical Christianity.

---

13. Francis Couvares, *Interpretations of American History Vol. I: Patterns and Perspectives* (New York: Simon and Schuster, 2000), p. 54.

14. J. Edwin Orr as quoted in Plueddemann, p. 6.

Chapter 9

PIETISM

Philipp Spener, the founder of Pietism, went to be with Christ early in 1705. A few days before he departed, he said, "During my life I have sufficiently lamented the condition of the church; now that I am about to enter the church triumphant, I wish to be buried in a white coffin as a sign I am dying in the hope of a better church on earth."[1]

The church that Spener left was certainly better off when he died than when he was born. In fact, the church at the time of Spener's birth (some one hundred years after Luther posted

1. As quoted by Aeron Morgan, *The Hope of a Better Church* (Wellington, New Zealand: CWM ministries, 2001), p. 1. Accessed at http://www.christian-witness.org/archives/van2000/offcross5.html on Monday, April 7, 2014.

the ninety-five theses), was characterized by theological disputes, moral laxity, and spiritual dryness. God chose Spener to speak into this bleak situation.

Although his biblical preaching transformed lives, Spener's main contribution was his pen. Spener's book, *Pia Desideria,* set forth reforms that touched every level of society. Countless books were written on the same theme before and after Spener. None of them, however, approached *Pia Desideria* in its conciseness and clarity of thought. All the ideas and all the proposals for a reform of existing conditions had been present again and again before him. Yet nobody but Spener was capable of putting them together in the way in which we find them in the *Pia Desideria.*

BACKGROUND OF THE TIMES

In the sixteenth and seventeenth centuries, the church had turned to the German princes as their protectors and esteemed members. State churches were managed by rulers and all citizens of the country were automatically members. Richard Balge states,

> A kind of Caesaropapism had replaced the Roman Catholic hierarchy in Germany after the Reformation. The German princes, as 'the chief members of the church,' were asked to take the place of Catholic bishops as chief ecclesiastical administrators.[2]

2. Richard D. Balge, "Pietism's Teaching on Church and Ministry as Evidenced in its Pastoral Practice," Essay by Professor Emeritus Wisconsin Lutheran Seminary. as quoted in James W. Ptak, *Spener's Proposals to Correct Conditions in the Church as the Basis for the Evangelical Covenant Church's Affirmations*, Thesis for the Master of Arts in Religion (Charlotte, South Carolina: Reformed Theological Seminary, 2008), p. 25.

While it is hard to understand why the church depended so heavily on the political rulers, we can surmise that they wanted to avoid the same fate as the Waldensians, Hussites, and Lollards. Divergent religious movements at the time were routinely exterminated by armies loyal to the Roman Catholic Church. Frederick Herzog writes,

> The growth of the power of the princes in the affairs of the church was one of the major developments that led to the emergence of Pietism, however little Pietism itself may have been conscious of the problem. The Reformation simply had not come to grips with the relationship between the political and the religious spheres. To the extent that princes shaped the end result of the Reformation, interest in spirituality dwindled. This laid the actual ground for the subsequent attacks of Pietism on the corruption of the church.[3]

Much of Germany was devastated by the Catholic-Protestant conflict called the Thirty Years War (1618–1648). Famine and disease significantly decreased the population of the German states and most of the combatant powers were bankrupted. Many who went through the Thirty Years War felt blindsided and were desperate for change.

And the church didn't have the answers. Bickering between theologians turned off the laity, and Christianity itself was discredited by the violence of the religious wars. Ministers preached theological legalism that no one could, or wanted to, understand.[4] The church services were formal and sterile.

---

3. Frederick Herzog, *European Pietism Reviewed* (San Jose, CA: Pickwick Publications, 2003), p. 4.

4. Latham, p. 58.

Drunkenness and immorality was common among the clergy.[5] A rigid distinction existed between clergy and laity, which tended to motivate lay people even less. Other class distinctions were evident within the churches, such as elevated and upholstered seats that were reserved for the upper classes, while the common people sat on hard chairs in the nave.

Germans were Lutherans simply because they lived in Lutheran territory. Religion was a matter of geography. With the flame of the church burning dimly, people became interested in other things.

PHILIPP JAKOB SPENER

Philipp Spener was born in 1635. He was trained by a devout godmother who developed his spiritual hunger by encouraging him to read devotional books like Johann Arndt's *True Christianity*, a book that emphasized personal holiness and devotion. Spener was a sharp student, and by the age of sixteen he entered the university where he studied under well-known Lutheran scholars. Spener was captivated by Luther, and later claimed that no other author since biblical times was so enlightened.

Spener then studied theology at Strasbourg, where the professors at the time (and especially Sebastian Schmidt) were more inclined to "practical" Christianity than to theological disputation. He afterwards spent a year in Geneva and was influenced by the strict moral life and ecclesiastical discipline prevalent there, and also by the preaching and the piety of the Waldensian professor, Antoine Leger, and the converted Jesuit preacher, Jean de Labadie. After graduation from class work, Spener took the customary two years of travel.

---

5. Latourette, p. 895.

In 1666, he was called to the pastorate in Frankfurt. He immediately began to espouse his spiritual views, which remained relatively unchanged over the next twenty-five years. He started to hold religious meetings at his home, which he called *collegia pietatis* (schools of piety or godliness). In these home groups, he would repeat his sermons, expound passages of the New Testament, and encourage those present to ask questions and apply Scripture.[6]

Spener led the first group in 1670 and then made rules and regulations for the new groups. He encouraged others to open their own homes to practice the priesthood of all believers, so that everyone would be involved. Pastors or professors served as qualified facilitators of these groups. Even though Spener's movement was eventually suppressed in his hometown of Frankfurt, it survived to influence the Moravians and Methodists, who in turn sparked the eighteenth century Great Awakening.[7]

PIA DESIDERIA

In 1675, Spener published his *Pia Desideria* (Godly Desires). The title *Pia* or *Pious* initiated the term *Pietists*. This was originally a derogatory term given to the adherents of the movement by its enemies as a form of ridicule. Influenced by earlier Pietistic writers in England and Germany, Spener took advantage of a Frankfurt publisher's invitation to write a preface for a new edition of Johann Arndt's *True Christianity* (1605).[8] Arndt had

6. Latourette, p. 895.

7. Molenaar, p. 34.

8. Spener was also deeply affected by the religious views of Countess Agathe. Her Christianity has been characterized as "world-fleeing, quietistic, even mystical." Spener also lists as a key influence, his parish pastor, Stoll, who was a strict Lutheran with a practical bent. There were several other

previously come to the conclusion that true Christianity comprised right thinking, living, and spiritual union of the soul with God. Arndt had already greatly influenced Spener and *Pia Desideria* amplified the themes of *True Christianity.*

As was his custom, Spener discussed his preface with his fellow ministers before submitting his manuscript in 1675. He dedicated his preface to all officials and pastors, and it won immediate acclaim, so much so that within six months he published the preface separately under its own title, *Pia Desideria.* In the book, he pinpointed the spiritual conditions he observed with a six point plan for church renewal. He addressed the "scandalous worldliness" of the churches and his hope for renewal based on first century Christianity. As a result of the book and Spener's own example, the movement called Pietism flourished. Donald Bloesch describes Pietism this way, "Among the salient features of Pietism is the emphasis upon the religion of the heart. . . . In the Pietist movement there is an existential emphasis, a call for personal involvement in the truth of the faith."[9]

In *Pia Desideria,* Spener exposed sins among the authorities, clergy, and laity. He cautions the clergy to stop trying to win debates and exhorts them to have a childlike heart that promotes the kingdom of God. His main critique of the clergy is that they have replaced the simple and clear preaching of the gospel with a morbid interest in controversial nit picking.

---

devotional authors who influenced Spener during this period: Emmanuel Sothom's *Golden Crown-Jewels of the Children of God* (which was written that "those who are Christian in name might become Christian also in deeds and in truth") and Lewis Bailey's *The Practice of Piety.*

9. Donald G. Bloesch, *The Evangelical Renaissance* (Grand Rapids, MI: Eerdmans Publishing Company, 1973), p. 106.

He believed that the clergy's one-sided impractical education led them to theoretical preaching that strengthened a false and illusory conception of what constitutes true faith. Spener then gets to the heart of *Pia Desideria,* offering six major proposals for church reform:

First proposal: The earnest and thorough study of the Bible in private meetings, *ecclesiolae in ecclesia* (little churches within the church). Spener proposed that the church renew Luther's emphasis on the priesthood of all believers through *collegia pietatis*. These were small interactive meetings of lay Christians who studied the Bible, encouraged one another, and prayed together. He writes,

> It would even be useful if we again brought into being the ancient apostolic way of gathering the church together . . . Instead of just one getting up to teach, which will still be done at other times, others who are blessed with talents and insight would also contribute. They would present their pious thoughts which might be instructive to the rest.

He cited 1 Corinthians 14 as the format and encouraged believers to open their homes. Spener argued that small groups were necessary because the people were not learning the Bible through the customary Sunday meetings. He wrote,

> The congregation does not hear the rest at all, or they hear only a few sayings or directives which are mentioned in the sermon without being able to understand their whole significance even though there is something important in them . . . The people have little opportunity to grasp the understanding of the Scripture in any other way than from the texts

> that are interpreted to them. That they even have less opportunity to use the Scriptures themselves as their edification requires.

Second proposal: Since the Christian priesthood was universal, the laity should share in the spiritual government of the church. Spener felt it necessary because,

> . . . one of the foremost reasons why the minister cannot accomplish everything and carry out what should be easy, is that he is too weak without the help of the universal priesthood of all believers. One man is not enough among so many since to just one is usually entrusted the accomplishment of everything necessary for the edification of the people under his care.

Third proposal: A knowledge of Christianity must have accompanying practice as its indispensable sign and supplement. Spener spoke about the insufficiency of knowledge alone. He said, "It is by no means enough to have knowledge of the Christian faith, for Christianity consists rather of practice."[10] He then goes on to quote the apostle John who consistently pointed to practice as characterizing true disciples of Jesus (John 13:34–35, 15:12 ; 1 John 3:10, 18, 4:7–8, 11–13, 21).

Fourth proposal: Instead of merely didactic, and often bitter attacks on unbelievers, he calls on his readers to have a loving attitude toward unbelievers. Spener believed Christians should win the person, rather than just the argument. The Christian ". . . should give no offense, whether it be from name calling,

---

10. Philip Jacob Spener (1964-01-01). *Pia Desideria* (p. 95). Fortress Press. Kindle Edition.

or an unloving lack of desire to win the disputant."[11] Spener thought that believers should realize the limitations of disputations and should accept those from other confessions.

Fifth proposal: A reorganization of the theological training of the universities, giving more prominence to the devotional life. Spener argued that the seminaries should choose only morally qualified students. An effort should be made to find out what their lives were like before they were admitted. Once there, the professors should supervise the lives of students, insisting on piety in addition to scholarship. They should terminate partying, joking around, and "rioting," and should even give certificates from the seminary stating that the graduate was qualified to minister because of his or her godly life.

Sixth proposal: A different style of preaching, namely, instead of pleasing rhetoric, the implanting of Christianity in the inner or new person, the soul of which is faith and the fruits of the Spirit. Spener proposed that existing clergy should preach sermons that encourage faith and fruit in the hearers. Sermons should be practical, focusing on inner change, as well as outer. No sermon should ever be devoid of application.

Spener's proposals produced an immediate response throughout Germany. While a large number of pastors adopted Spener's proposals, others were deeply offended by them.

SMALL GROUPS IN PIETISM

Many think of Pietism as a movement that helped individuals practice the personal spiritual disciplines. We must remember, however, that Spener originally wrote *Pia Desideria* to reform

---

11. Ibid., p. 100.

the church and to help move the church forward. Even the subtitle reflects this concern: *Heartfelt Desire for a God-pleasing Reform of the True Evangelical Church.* Granted, Spener proposed that each believer should study the Scripture in a personal way, but he also encouraged people to join church-sponsored small groups to grow in their faith. He wrote in *Pia Desideria*,

> For a third thing it would perhaps not be inexpedient (and I set this down for further and more mature reflection) to reintroduce the ancient and apostolic kind of church meetings. . . . Anybody who is not satisfied with his understanding of a matter should be permitted to express his doubts and seek further explanation. On the other hand, those (including the ministers) who have made more progress should be allowed the freedom to state how they understand each passage.[12]

Spener felt that this was the best way for people to experience spiritual growth and maturity. Spener feared that people who only heard God's Word would soon forget it without applying it and being transformed by it. He realized that without immediate application, biblical teaching could easily be lost in the busyness of life.[13] Donald F. Durnbaugh writes about one of the key differences in Pietism,

> The congregation was understood not so much as a vehicle for administering grace and the deposit of faith but rather as an association of the regenerate who came together to strengthen each other in the Christian walk. For this reason, a hallmark of Pietism

12. Spener, pp. 89-90.

13. Ibid., p. 90.

> came to be conventicles, small groups of earnest Christians who met privately for mutual edification and encouragement, the so-called *ecclesiola in ecclesia* (the little church within the church). Given this ecclesiastical understanding, it is not surprising that separatist movements arose, eventually discarding their allegiance to the state church.[14]

If the entire church was to be renewed, it needed to start with the serious Christians in each congregation. Spener never intended, however that the little churches within the church would replace the institutional church.

LEADERSHIP

Spener felt it was important for a qualified leader to be present in the home meetings in order to avoid false doctrine. This person normally was a pastor or a professor who was willing to take responsibility for the group.[15] However, the leader was not to dominate the discussion. Rather, he was to stir up participation among those who were present. Spener writes,

> The professor, as the leader, should reinforce good observations. If he sees, however, that students are departing from the end in view, he should proceed in clear and friendly fashion to set them right on the basis of the text and show them what opportunity they have to put this or that rule of conduct into practice.[16]

---

14. As quoted in Hans Schneider, *German Radical Pietism* (Lanham, Maryland: Scarecrow Press, 2007), p. vii.

15. Latham, p. 67.

16. Spener, p. 113.

His main objective was for each member of the group to participate, express thoughts, raise doubts, but to above all grow in maturity and holiness. He didn't want one person to dominate the meeting, while everyone else once again became listeners of a sermon.

MAINTAING BALANCE

Spener was very careful to include his small group emphasis within Lutheran ecclesiology and thus avoid the exclusivity of Anabaptism. Like Luther, he was part of the state church and his goal was to make the state church more holy and Christlike through small groups. The groups were supposed to supplement the Sunday morning worship service—not to replace it. He did not allow the people to call the groups "the true church," because he wanted to avoid doctrinal conflict.[17] Nor did Spener allow the celebration of the sacraments at the small group meetings. Communion was reserved for the entire congregation only.[18] On Sunday morning, he would often urge the congregation to participate in the small groups and to fulfill their Christian duties. Rather than play cards, he exhorted them to review the Sunday sermon in a small group.[19]

MEETINGS AND MATERIALS

Initially, the meetings were held in Spener's home every Wednesday and Sunday. The groups would meet for one hour. Both men and women were invited to attend. In Spener's initial

---

17. Doyle L. Young, *New Life For Your Church* (Grand Rapids, MI: Baker Book House, 1989), p. 109.

18. Young, p. 108.

19. Spener, p. 13.

home meeting, Lewis Bayly's *Practice of Piety* was used as a basis for the discussion.[20] However, in subsequent meetings, the Bible became the regular reference and foundation for further discussion, and the sermon text became the theme for the lessons. Spener was primarily concerned with Biblical application in the meetings, rather than Bible knowledge.[21] Besides Scripture application, prayer and hymn singing were important elements of the meetings.

Yet, Spener repeatedly stressed that the home meeting was not a substitute for one's personal devotional life. He only wanted people to come together who had already spent time in private Bible study and prayer. Throughout his *Pia Desideria*, the theme of private devotions and personal holiness appear again and again.

BRINGING BACK THE PRIESTHOOD

Luther talked about the priesthood of all believers but never really practiced it. Spener wanted to change this. Throughout *Pia Desidiera,* Spener quotes Luther, knowing that Luther was highly esteemed:

> Our frequently mentioned Dr. Luther would suggest another means, which is altogether compatible with the first. This second proposal is the establishment and diligent exercise of the spiritual priesthood. Nobody can read Luther's writings with some care without observing how earnestly the sainted man advocated this spiritual priesthood, according to which not only

20. Latham, p. 62.

21. Spener, p. 113.

> ministers but all Christians are made priests by their Savior, are anointed by the Holy Spirit, and are dedicated to perform spiritual-priestly acts.[22]

Spener always spoke very highly of Martin Luther, knowing that his hearers were fully committed to Lutheran teaching. Spener himself highly respected Martin Luther, although he also realized that many of Luther's teachings (including the priesthood of all believers) were not being practiced. On the other hand, Spener openly criticized the Catholic Church, highlighting both their hierarchical structure and how the average lay person was not able to truly practice the priesthood of all believers. He writes,

> Indeed, it was by a special trick of the cursed devil that things were brought to such a pass in the papacy that all these spiritual functions were assigned solely to the clergy (to whom alone the name "spiritual," which is in actual fact common to all Christians, was therefore arrogantly allotted) and the rest of the Christians were excluded from them, as if it were not proper for laymen diligently to study in the Word of the Lord, much less to instruct, admonish, chastise, and comfort their neighbors, or to do privately what pertains to the ministry publicly, inasmuch as all these things were supposed to belong only to the office of the minister . . . This presumptuous monopoly of the clergy, alongside the aforementioned prohibition of Bible reading, is one of the principal means by which papal Rome established its power over poor Christians and still preserves it wherever it has opportunity. The papacy could suffer no greater injury than having

22. Ibid., pp. 92-93.

> Luther point out that all Christians have been called to exercise spiritual functions (although not called to the public exercise of them, which requires appointment by a congregation with equal right) and that they are not only permitted but, if they wish to be Christians, are obligated to undertake them.[23]

The priesthood of the laity was not actively practiced, so he had to help the hearers understand that one pastor or priest is incapable of doing all that is necessary for the edification of the many persons who are generally entrusted to his pastoral care.[24]

A RETURN TO THE PAST

Spener refers often to primitive Christianity as a model for church reform. He extols the early house churches, the priesthood of all believers, and the spiritual life in the New Testament church. He writes, "It is the same Holy Spirit who is bestowed on us by God who once effected all things in the early Christians, and he is neither less able nor less active today to accomplish the work of sanctification in us."[25]

Spener believed God could do the same things in his day like was done after Pentecost, although realizing it would look different in his own day and age. Robert Moylan sums up the goal of Pietism in this way,

> It was the intention of classic Pietism to recapture, as far as possible, the essence and power of the "primitive

23. Spener, pp. 93-94.

24. Ibid., pp. 94-95.

25. Spener, p. 85.

> church"—the church of the first and second centuries. The Pietists seem to have concluded that it could best be achieved through what has become recognized as the theme of the pietistic renewal movement: "Change the church by changing the individual."[26]

Knowing the resistance toward Anabaptism and any type of separatism, Spener kept insisting that the small group meetings were in response to members of his congregation and remained under his own pastoral supervision.[27]

CRITICISMS OF SPENER'S REFORMS

The *Pia Desideria* was well received in Lutheran Germany with letters being written in defense of this book. But Spener was severely criticized for his idea of *collegia pietatis*, or small groups. Some of the opposition arose at Frankfurt because some who attended the small group meetings did not attend the public worship services and did not partake in the Lord's Supper.[28] Balthasar Mentzer, a superintendent from Darmstadt, thought these small groups were unbiblical and filled with erring spirits. It was Mentzer's influence as a superintendent that caused the first decree to be issued against the Pietists. However, there was never a charge against Spener himself, only his followers.[29]

---

26. Moylan, p. 156.

27. Frederick Herzog, *European Pietism Reviewed* (San Jose, CA: Pickwick Publications, 2003), p. 25.

28. Latourette, p. 895.

29. James W. Ptak, "Spener's Proposals to Correct Conditions in the Church as the Basis for the Evangelical Covenant Church's Affirmations," Thesis for the Master of Arts in Religion (Charlotte, South Carolina: Reformed Theological Seminary, 2008), p. 21.

Some felt that the Pietists were not sufficiently concerned with integrity, morality, and virtue, but were overly concerned about their relationship with God.[30] Others felt that the Pietists were far too emotional.[31] The authorities within the state-endorsed church became suspicious of Pietistic doctrine, which they viewed as a social danger. They didn't like the evangelical fervor that disturbed the public tranquility and obscured the imperatives of morality.

The constant opposition toward Pietism did hinder Spener's reforms. In Frankfurt, a suspicious city council ordered the small group meetings to be closed down.[32] The criticisms eventually wore upon Spener and by 1703 (thirty-three years after the beginning of the small groups) Spener had become cynical and cautious about small group reforms. Criticisms of Spener eventually forced him out of Saxony in the 1690s, and he went to Brandenburg, where he helped start the University of Halle. In spite of all the struggles, Spener's movement became the forerunner of the Moravians, Methodists, and ultimately the modern day cell church movement.

THE SPREAD OF PIETISM

Spener died in 1705, but the movement continued, guided by one of Spener's disciples, August Hermann Francke (1663-1727). Through Spener's influence, Francke was able to obtain a teaching post at the University of Halle, which later became a chief center of Pietism. Latourette says about Francke, "He

---

30. Harry Yeide, Jr., *Studies in Classical Pietism* (New York: Peter Lang Publishing, 1997), pp. 4-5.

31. Peter C. Erb, editor, *Pietists: Selected Writings* (New York: Paulist Press, 1983), p. 8.

32. Young, p. 109.

was the dominant figure on the theological faculty and in the training of young men for the ministry. A faithful pastor in his own parish, he brought to his lecture room not only theory but also practical experience."[33]

Francke was a brilliant scholar, but he also was very concerned about living a godly life. He established orphanages, promoted foreign missions, and Christian good works. Francke stressed repeatedly the importance of having Scriptures in one's heart, not just in the head. According to Francke, it was necessary to have small group meetings alongside the regular church service. Many Lutheran churches began to practice his principles. However, opposition increased to the point that Francke was forced to resign his teaching post.[34] Yet from Halle, missionaries were sent forth who promoted Pietism around the world.

Among Pietism's greatest achievements was the revival of the Moravian Church in 1727 by Count von Zinzendorf, Spener's godson and a pupil in the Halle School for Young Noblemen. Zinzendorf was strongly influenced by Pietism while at Halle. Zinzendorf in turn influenced John Wesley. As Sohn declares, "Missiologically speaking, it [Pietism] formed part of the launching pad of Protestant World Mission."[35]

---

33. Latourette, p. 896.

34. Ibid., p. 896.

35. Damien Sangwoong Sohn, *A Missio-Historical Analysis of German Lutheran Pietism in the Seventeenth Century* M.A. thesis (Pasadena, CA: Fuller Theological Seminary, 1990), p. 50.

LESSONS LEARNED

- Spener's early years prepared him for later ministry. His reading of Arndt and other likeminded authors prepared Spener to influence history.
- Spener employed both writing and practice to shake up the traditional clergy and start a movement.
- Spener's small groups emphasized participation, spiritual disciplines, community, and the application of the Sunday sermon. The small groups were never a substitute for personal devotions and private Bible study. Although he appointed leaders (perhaps overly qualified leaders), these leaders were instructed not to dominate the discussion but to allow group members to freely participate.
- It's evident from Pietism that change takes time and is often resisted. Even after thirty years of implementing change, many in Germany resisted Pietism, and eventually Spener left the pastorate in Frankfurt.
- Spener developed disciples who carried on his philosophy to successive generations—specifically through teaching these reforms in the university, which gave students new ideas and the necessary tools to put them into practice. Spener's life teaches us that what we do today might not affect our own generation as much as future ones.

Chapter 10

THE MORAVIANS

On August 27, 1727, a prayer meeting started that lasted one hundred years. It began on Count Zinzendorf's property known as "Under the Lord's Watch." Twenty-four men and twenty-four women committed themselves to spend an hour each day in around the clock prayer. Soon others joined the prayer chain. Days passed, then months. Unceasing prayer rose to God twenty-four-hours a day as someone—at least one—was engaged in intercessory prayer each hour of every day. The intercessors met weekly for encouragement and to read letters and messages from their brothers in different places, giving them specific needs to pray about. It was a prayer meeting that lasted over one hundred years.

Undoubtedly this prayer chain helped birth Protestant missions. Six months into it, Zinzendorf suggested the possibility of attempting to reach others for Christ in the West Indies, Greenland, Turkey, and Lapland. Twenty-six Moravians stepped forward the next day to volunteer. The first missionaries, Leonard Dober and David Nitschmann, were commissioned on August 18, 1732, during which one hundred hymns were sung. During the first two years, twenty-two missionaries perished and two more were imprisoned, but others took their places. Seventy Moravian missionaries were sent forth from the six hundred inhabitants of Herrnhut.

By the time William Carey became the "Father of Modern Missions," over three hundred Moravian missionaries had already gone to the ends of the earth. The Moravian fervor sparked the conversions of John and Charles Wesley and indirectly ignited the Great Awakening that swept through Europe and America. The prayer meeting lasted one hundred years, but the results will last for eternity.[1]

NIKOLAUS ZINZENDORF

Zinzendorf was both a godly man and a wealthy one. Born into Austrian nobility and raised by his grandmother, Zinzendorf showed an early inclination toward theology and religious work. His parents left him in the hands of a godly grandmother, who trained him and sent him to study at Halle University. While at Halle, he was swept up in the teachings of Pietism.

---

1. Robert J. Morgan, *On This Day* (Nashville: Thomas Nelson Publishers, 1997) as quoted in Matthew Kratz, "The 100-Year Prayer Meeting," http://www.sermoncentral.com/illustrations/sermon-illustration-matthew-kratz-stories-63793.asp

Zinzendorf's brand of Pietism was pure theology of the heart. He also added the feature of evangelism, which was lacking in Pietistic teachings.

Zinzendorf believed that Christianity should be experienced and not just taught. He emphasized the experience of faith and love, and was more accepting of varying denominational differences. In fact, Zinzendorf may have been the first churchman to use the word *ecumenism*. The Moravians also placed special importance on community through small groups.

His theology was profoundly Christ-centered, and he often emphasized the growth of the spiritual relationship between the believer and the Savior. He believed that Christians should live in radical love and harmony, and that every believer needed to live in a faith community. Decisions on interpretation of Scripture were to be made communally, not individually. Zinzendorf's theology included the emotional life of the believer as well as the intellectual. He referred to this as the "religion of the heart."

OFFERING REFUGE

Following his marriage in 1722 to Countess Erdmuth Dorothea von Reuss, Zinzendorf began his work in the court at Dresden and moved to his estate at Berthelsdorf near the Bohemian border of Saxony. In that same year, Christian David, a leader among the group of ancient Hussites (followers of John Hus), approached Count Zinzendorf about the difficult plight of his people and the possibility of relocating some of them to Zinzendorf's property. Christian David knew that Zinzendorf was compassionate, wealthy, and lived in close proximity to the Hussites, who were later named *United Brethren*. The Count also received a petition from the exiles,

> We are under great concern, lest we should be burdensome to you with this building. We most humbly entreat you to take us into your gracious protection, to assist us, poor, afflicted, and simple people, and to treat us with kindness and affection. We will entreat Almighty God to bless you in body and soul for so doing . . . .[2]

Zinzendorf agreed to house the refugees, and that same year, the first ten Moravian United Brethren arrived. They named it *the Lord's watch* (*Herrnhut*) and immediately began construction.

In the beginning, Zinzendorf didn't fully understand the historic connection between the United Brethren and John Hus. It wasn't until Zinzendorf discovered a copy of their fifteenth century constitution and realized that the United Brethren predated Lutheranism and were already a fully established church. Even more amazing were the similarities between the vision and values of Zinzendorf and this group of Hussites. Zinzendorf realized that this connection could be a spark for renewal for the church in general.

After five years, Zinzendorf left the Dresden court to concentrate on shepherding the growing settlement, which now had a population of about three hundred. Over the doorway of Zinzendorf's house at Herrnhut, he had inscribed these lines:

> As guests we only here remain;
> And hence this house is slight and plain.

---

2. Rev. August Gottlieb Spangenberg, *The Life of Nicholas Lewis Count Zinzendorf* (London: Samuel Holdsworth, 1838), p. 39.

We have a better house above,
And there we fix our warmest love.[3]

John Wesley later visited the Count's house and described it as a small, plain building like the rest; having a large garden behind it, well laid out, not for show, but for the use of the community.

THE BANDS

Officially, the division of the Herrnhut refugees into smaller groups referred to as "bands" and eventually "choirs" began in July 1727, five years after the first refugees arrived. However, the United Brethren practiced these small group meetings even before arriving at Herrnhut.[4] The bands grew rapidly, and in 1732 there were seventy-seven bands, and by 1734 there were one hundred.[5]

The purpose of these small groups of three to eight people was to promote growth in grace and fellowship. They met frequently for prayer and intimate discussion of personal experiences. Each member of the congregation could join the band most congenial to him or her. The bands met daily for worship and discussion. They met in the leader's room, at work, under a tree, or wherever the Spirit moved them to meet. The

---

3. A. J. Lewis, *Zinzendorf the Ecumenical Pioneer* (London: SCM Press Ltd., 1962), p. 164. Zechariah 9:12 and 2 Corinthians 5:1-2 were also cited but not written out.

4. Kenneth G. Hamilton and F. Taylor, *History of the Moravian Church* (Bethlehem, PA: Moravian Church in America, 1967), p. 32.

5. David Lowes Watson, *The Early Methodist Class Meeting* (Nashville, TN: Discipleship Resources, 1987), p. 78.

groups encouraged confession, spiritual growth, community discipline, and character building. Zinzendorf moved freely among the groups, speaking to them, praying or singing with them, and offering general oversight. Sometimes Zinzendorf planned his visit, and at other times they were impromptu.[6]

Zinzendorf himself was the greatest supporter of the bands. Referring to the bands, he wrote, "I believe without such an institution, the church would never have become what it is now."[7] The bands gradually changed over time and morphed into a more formal "choir" system, which was based upon age, sex, and marital status.

THE CHOIRS

As the Moravian Church developed, the people were divided into choirs according to age, sex and marital status. Each choir had approximately ten to twenty-five people. They developed choirs for widowers, widows, married people, single men, single women, older boys, older girls, younger boys, and younger girls. Each group had its own meetings, activities, and the adult groups lived together in their own houses.[8] F. Taylor and K. Hamilton note, "In time the voluntary associations cultivated in the band were supplanted by compulsory membership in the choir."[9]

---

6. John R. Weinlick, *Count Zinzendorf* (New York: Abingdon Press, 1956), p. 84.

7. David Lowes Watson, p. 78.

8. Hamilton and Taylor, p. 37.

9. Ibid., p. 37.

Zinzendorf felt that the merits of Christ applied in a mysterious way to specific age and homogeneous groups. He formed the choir system to implement this spiritual principle. Zinzendorf took advantage of this homogeneity to speak to each group according to their specific needs.

Each choir had their own service, but also attended a larger gathering consisting of all the groups. The choirs were also divided into bands (three to eight people), which met for prayer, song, and testimony.[10] One key reason for the choirs was to promote singing and active participation by the congregation in worship. Zinzendorf promoted an appreciation of the spiritual power of hymnody and even developed a special type of service that was totally dedicated to public worship.[11] The goal of the choir groups was spiritual growth.

The choirs participated in the economic and educational development of the Moravian community. Houses were built for the specific choirs, and these choirs were instrumental in supporting the missionary movement.[12] Sessler writes about life for the Moravians in America in the year 1748,

> The older girls were then in Bethlehem, and the younger girls in Nazareth, while the small boys were on Henry Antes' farm. The married men and the married women lived separately in two buildings a short distance north of where the church in Bethlehem now stands. Even the children of pre-school age were

10. Jacob John Sessler, *Communal Pietism Among Early American Moravians* (New York: Henry Holt & Company, 1933), p. 98.

11. Hamilton and Taylor, p. 37.

12. Sessler, p. 94.

> taken charge of by the church. Supposedly these conditions of the choir were temporary.[13]

Each choir member received a daily visit from someone else in the choir to provide encouragement and determine the state of his or her soul. They felt the need to assess the spiritual condition of each member. Members were then identified as "dead," "awakened," "ignorant," "willing disciples," or "disciples that have made progress." It's interesting that similar terminology appears in early Methodist class meeting papers.

Shepherds or elders supervised the choirs and visited them regularly to care for their spiritual and physical needs. David Watson writes,

> In practice, the whole congregation came under a religious discipline to the extent that the officers of the community concerned themselves with spiritual as well as physical welfare, elders being appointed to keep watch over the maintenance of good order and discipline under the authority of two wardens, one of whom was the Count himself.[14]

Zinzendorf was able to organize his refugees into something like a Christian military regime. However, he didn't establish his movement around the traditional nuclear family of parents and children. Rather, he was primarily focused on communal families based on age, marital status and gender. Jacob Sessler gives a clear picture of these groups,

---

13. Ibid., p. 94.

14. David Lowes Watson, p. 77.

> From the earliest years children were taught that they belonged more to the church than to their parents. They became the property of the church, and it was expected that when they grew up they should serve the institution which had nurtured and cared for them in their childhood and adolescence. The basis for the wide-spread mission work of the Moravians is found chiefly in their firm belief that the church had first claim on their lives. . . . When later they were called upon to go into distant mission fields, their past training made it easier for them, since they had very few parental and home ties to break.[15]

PRIMITIVE CHRISTIANITY

Benjamin Ingham, wrote about the Herrnhut community,

> They are more like the Primitive Christians than any other church now in the world, for they retain both the faith, practice and discipline delivered by the Apostles. They live together in perfect love and peace. They are more ready to serve their neighbors than themselves. In their business they are diligent and industrious, in all their dealings strictly just and conscientious. In everything they behave themselves with great meekness, sweetness and simplicity.[16]

Like Spener's Pietistic groups, the Moravian communities were *ecclesiolae in ecclesia* (little churches within the church), whose

15. Sessler, pp. 98-99.

16. Joseph Edmund Hutton (2011-03-24). *A History of the Moravian Church* (Kindle Locations 3770-3778). Kindle Edition.

purpose was to renew the whole church.[17] Other reformers before Zinzendorf viewed the house churches as essential, but Zinzendorf practiced in a new way the concept of the church within the church. In his doctoral dissertation on small group renewal, William Brown states,

> Perhaps one of the most deliberate and successful uses of the small group principle in church history is the band system of Count Zinzendorf in the middle of the eighteenth century. The micro communities of Herrnhut combined the aspects of fellowship and sharing, mutual correction and confession, prayer and an urgent sense of mission to send the gospel to the world and bring renewal to Christians. They made use of lay leadership and literally followed the kind of meeting advised in James 5:13-16.[18]

Luther longed for a return to primitive Christianity through small groups but was unable to practice it. Spener was bolder and even implemented groups but hesitated when the criticism came. Francke, a university president was not the one to apply the church within a church. Yet, Zinzendorf had the authority to actually practice church renewal through small groups and then send those groups to do worldwide church planting.

SENDING THE GROUPS AROUND THE WORLD

Zinzendorf once said, "To be a brother and to promote the work of the heathen mission: they are one and the same

---

17. Young, p. 110.

18. Brown, p. 38.

thing."[19] His zeal for the mission was seen in his student days at Halle University, where he led missionary prayer times. God answered those prayers by sending him a diverse group of Separatists, Reformed, Lutherans, Catholics, and other persecuted groups who came to live at Herrnhut. They learned to work together, respect the Lutheran church (for the sake of the authorities), and also recognize the special role of the Unity of the Brethren movement.[20] God was preparing them to work together in unity as they were sent out as missionaries to reach the nations and change the world.

While visiting Copenhagen in 1731, Zinzendorf met Anthony Ulrich, a converted slave from the West Indies. He was looking for someone to go back to his homeland to preach the gospel to black slaves, which included his sister and brother. Zinzendorf raced back to Herrnhut to find men to go and two immediately volunteered, becoming the first Moravian missionaries—and the first Protestant missionaries of the modern era, antedating William Carey by sixty-some years.

Another major mission moment came in 1733 when the Saxony government refused to allow any more refugees to settle on Zinzendorf's estate. Zinzendorf realized that he needed to decentralize and expand his mission base. By 1736, relations with the government of Saxony had deteriorated to such an extent that Zinzendorf was forced into exile for a number of years. He used this time away from Herrnhut to help create other communities, notably in America. He was even willing to become a bishop of the Moravian church when it became

---

19. Harry Yeide, Jr., *Studies in Classical Pietism* (New York: Peter Lang Publishing, 1997), p. 73.

20. Ibid., p. 70.

impossible to start missionary churches without an organized church structure. It was through this new church structure that many missionaries were sent around the world.[21]

The missionary work in the West Indies had been hugely controversial in Europe, with many accusing Zinzendorf of simply sending young missionaries off to die. Zinzendorf decided to place himself on the line, and in 1739 he left Europe to visit the mission work on Saint Thomas.

Convinced that he himself might not come back, he preached his "last sermon" and left his will with his wife. The visit was a huge success, however, and enabled him to free some of the missionaries who had been illegally jailed. God even used the mistreatment of the Moravian missionaries to garner respect among the slaves.

In 1741, Zinzendorf visited Pennsylvania, becoming one of the few eighteenth century European nobles to visit the Americas. He also visited leaders in Philadelphia, such as Benjamin Franklin, met with the leaders of the Iroquois, and reached agreements to ensure free movement of Moravian missionaries in the area.

Missionary colonies were settled in the West Indies (1732), in Greenland (1733), among the North American Indians (1735), and before Zinzendorf's death, the Moravians had established missionary colonies in Livonia, South Carolina, Suriname, several parts of South America, Tranquebar, Nicobar Islands in the East Indies, Egypt, Labrador, and the west coast of South

---

21. Gillian Lindt Gollin, *Moravians in Two Worlds* (New York: Columbia University Press, 1967), p. 5.

Africa. In these communities, a radical equality of spiritual life was practiced. For example, in Bethlehem, PA nobility and converted native Americans shared common quarters; in Salem, slaves were full members of the church and could be elected to offices of leadership. By 1760 the Moravians had sent out two hundred twenty-six foreign missionaries.[22]

DECLINING YEARS

The community in Herrnhut, from which almost all these colonies had been sent out, had no money of its own, and Zinzendorf had almost exclusively paid its expenses. His frequent journeys from home made it difficult for him to look after his private affairs. He was compelled from time to time to raise money by loans, and in 1750, he was almost bankrupt. This led to the establishment of a financial board among the Brethren to administrate financial matters of the Moravian movement and to ensure its stability.

In 1756 Zinzendorf lost his wife, Erdmuthe Dorothea, who had been his counselor and confidante in all his work. Zinzendorf remained a widower for one year, and then married Anna Caritas Nitschmann with whom he had been very close for many years. Three years later, he fell ill and died in 1760, leaving Bishop Johannes von Watteville, who had married his eldest daughter Benigna, to take his place at the head of the community.

Zinzendorf's influence reverberated far beyond the Moravian church. His emphasis on the "religion of the heart" deeply influenced John Wesley. He is remembered today, as Karl

---

22. Yeide, p. 75.

Barth put it, as "perhaps the only genuine Christocentric of the modern age." Scholar George Forell put it more succinctly: Zinzendorf was "the noble Jesus freak."[23] He's remembered for his small group creativity, but even more importantly how he mobilized those groups to fulfill Christ's great commission through worldwide missionary outreach.

LESSONS LEARNED

- The Moravian small groups (both bands and choirs) were very creative and contemporary for their time.
- Moravians were exemplary for their prayer emphasis. Prayer vigils and prayer chains met around the clock. Each person spent his or her time in intercession, so that prayer never ceased in the community.
- Community was an essential component that stands out in the Moravian movement. Zinzendorf believed in experiencing the Christian life, both individually but also communally. He felt it was important to live in harmony and oneness with others as an essential spiritual component. Zinzendorf once said, "I do not establish Christianity without community,"[24]
- Moravian choirs often separated children from parents and parents from children—for the cause of Christ's church.

---

23. Taken from article entitled, "Nikolaus von Zinzendorf," at http://www.christianitytoday.com/ch/131christians/denominationalfounders/zinzendorf.html?start=1. Accessed on Monday, December 16, 2013.

24. Heikki Lempa and Paul Peucker, eds. *Self, Community, World: Moravian Education in a Transatlantic World* (Bethlehem, PA: Leheigh University Press, 2010), p. 23.

- The dynamic connection between small groups and missions is the lasting legacy of the Moravians. The emphasis on missions helped the groups adapt to culture and different circumstances. We're reminded of the Celtic bands in the Middle Ages that allowed people to belong and then believe.

Chapter 11

JOHN WESLEY, FOUNDER OF METHODISM

In 1928 Archbishop Davidson wrote, "Wesley practically changed the outlook and even the character of the English nation."[1] The Wesleyan revival cut across denominational lines and touched every level of society. England itself was

1. As quoted in Diane Severance, "Evangelical Revival in England," Christianity.com, http://www.christianity.com/church/church-history/timeline/1701-1800/evangelical-revival-in-england-11630228.html, p. 1. Accessed on Friday, April 11, 2014.

transformed by the revival. The revival so altered the course of English history that it probably saved England from the kind of revolution that took place in France.

England before the Methodist movement was described as a moral quagmire and a spiritual cesspool. Thomas Carlyle used the phrase "Stomach well alive, soul extinct" to describe the conditions in England.[2] Drunkenness was rampant; gambling was so extensive that one historian described England as "one vast casino." Newborns were exposed in the streets; ninety-seven percent of the infant poor in the workhouses died as children. Bear baiting and cock fighting were acceptable sports, and tickets were sold publically for these events. The slave trade brought material gain to many while further degrading their own lives. Bishop Berkeley wrote that morality and religion in Britain had collapsed "to a degree that was never known in any Christian country."[3]

The industrial Revolution made people feel like machines, and the result of the economic turmoil were slum conditions that produced poor tenements in crowded municipalities, with bad hygiene, poor health, and the absence of any real sense of community for a large section of the population.[4] Henderson writes,

> One of the most demoralizing vices of the poor was wide-spread alcoholism, even among the children. In 1736 every sixth house in London was licensed as a grogshop. Gin consumption topped eleven million gallons a year in England alone. This epidemic

---

2. Ibid., p. 1.

3. Ibid., p. 1.

4. David Lowes Watson, p. 130.

> of drunkenness eroded what little decency was left among the working people, leaving them adrift in hopeless despair.[5]

The Anglican Church was dead and dying. David Lowes Watson writes:

> Churches were subsidized by the government, and pastors were paid "livings" from state tax revenues. Of the 11,000 "livings" in 1750, 6,000 were occupied by men who never set foot in their own parishes; they lived in London or on the continent and farmed their parishes out to the poorly-paid, under-trained curates. Very few paid any concern to their pastorates, especially in those districts from which the industrial workers came.[6]

Into these conditions walks John Wesley. To bring about the spiritual changes, John Wesley travelled some two hundred fifty thousand miles (mainly on horseback), preached more than forty thousand sermons (two or three times each day), and gave away some thirty thousand English pounds from his own book earnings. He formed societies, opened chapels, examined and commissioned preachers, administered aid charities, prescribed for the sick, and superintended schools and orphanages. Wesley used all the profits from his literary works for charitable purposes, and he encouraged Christians to become active in social reform.

He spoke out strongly against the slave trade and encouraged William Wilberforce in his antislavery crusade. Numerous

---

5. D. Michael Henderson, *John Wesley's Class Meeting* (Nappanee, IN: Evangel Publishing House, 1997), p. 19.

6. Henderson, p. 20.

Christian aid societies arose as a result of the Methodist revival. Hospitals and schools multiplied. By the turn of the century, the movement Wesley started, called Methodism, had reached one hundred thousand members and established ten thousand classes (small groups). This system of bands and classes continued for over a century.[7] Hundreds of thousands of people participated in the small group system.[8]

John Wesley and Methodism significantly moved forward the concept and practice of small groups. Wesley's small groups emphasized transparency, holiness, evangelism, and multiplication. He also gathered those groups into larger gatherings, foreshadowing the modern day cell church. For these reasons, I decided to dedicate two chapters to Methodism—one focused on its founder, John Wesley, and the other to the small groups within Methodism.

WESLEY'S UPBRINGING

John Wesley was born in 1703 in Epworth, England. He was the fifteenth child of Samuel and Susanna Wesley. Samuel Wesley was a graduate of the University of Oxford and a Church of England rector. Wesley's parents had both become members of the established Church of England early in adulthood, although they also had a strong Puritan heritage. Susanna bore Samuel Wesley nineteen children, but only nine lived. In 1696, Samuel was appointed the rector of Epworth.

7. Howard Snyder, *The Radical Wesley and Patterns for Church Renewal* (Downers Grove, IL: InterVarsity Press, 1980), p. 62. From 1738 to 1798 the movement grew from zero to 149 circuits with 101,712 members.

8. Brown, p. 39.

As in many families at the time, Wesley's parents practiced "home schooling" during the early years of their children's development. Each child, including the girls, was taught to read as soon as he or she could walk and talk. They were expected to become proficient in Latin and Greek and to have learned major portions of the New Testament by heart. Susanna Wesley examined each child before the midday meal and prior to evening prayers. Children were not allowed to eat between meals and were interviewed by their mother one evening each week for the purpose of intensive spiritual instruction. From an early age, God in his sovereignty prepared Wesley for small group ministry. Plueddeman writes,

> His own mother, Susanna, had initiated home meetings in the parsonage years before. These began with devotional times which Susanna led for her children. A few neighbors asked to attend, and eventually the group grew to over 200 people, . . . the vision for home groups would become an important dynamic in the ministry of her sons, John and Charles.[9]

In 1714, at age eleven, Wesley was sent to the Charterhouse School in London (under the mastership of John King from 1715), where he lived the studious, methodical and—for a while—religious life in which he had been trained at home.

OXFORD

In June 1720, Wesley entered Christ Church, Oxford. By 1724, Wesley had graduated with a Bachelor of Arts degree but then decided to pursue a degree of Master of Arts. He was ordained a deacon on September 25, 1725 and also became a fellow and

9. Plueddemann, p. 8.

tutor at the university. In that same year, he read Thomas á Kempis and Jeremy Taylor and began to personally seek God for revival. The reading of William Law's *Christian Perfection* and *A Serious Call to a Devout and Holy Life* gave him a better understanding of the law of God. Wesley resolved to keep it, inwardly and outwardly, as sacredly as possible, believing that in obedience he would find salvation. He pursued a rigidly methodical and self-denying lifestyle. He daily studied the Scriptures, performed spiritual disciplines, and deprived himself of physical pleasures so that he would have more alms to give.

In March 1726, Wesley was unanimously elected a fellow of Lincoln College, Oxford. This carried with it the right to a room at the college and regular salary. While continuing his studies, Wesley taught Greek, lectured on the New Testament, and moderated academic debates at the university. However, in the midst of his academic career, he felt called to the ministry.

In August 1727, after taking his master's degree, Wesley returned to Epworth because his father requested his assistance in serving the neighboring parish of Wroote. Ordained an Anglican priest on September 22, 1728, Wesley served as an associate priest for two years. He returned to Oxford in November 1729 to maintain his status as junior fellow.

During Wesley's absence, his younger brother Charles matriculated at Christ College. When John returned, they formed a small club for the purpose of study and the pursuit of a devout Christian life. John became the leader of the group, and it increased in number and commitment (George Whitefield became a part of this club). The group met daily from six until nine for prayer, reading the Psalms, and studying the Greek New Testament. They also fasted on Wednesdays and Fridays until three o'clock, as was commonly observed in the ancient church. They preached, educated the unlearned, relieved jailed debtors whenever possible, and cared for the sick.

Given the low ebb of spirituality in Oxford at that time, Wesley's group provoked a negative reaction. They were considered to be religious "fanatics." University wits coined the term "holy club," a title of derision. The opposition intensified following the mental breakdown and death of a group member, William Morgan. In response to the charge that "rigorous fasting" had hastened his death, Wesley noted that Morgan had stopped fasting 1.5 years earlier. In the same widely circulated letter, Wesley referred to the name "Methodist" saying that certain ones were pleased to compliment the club with that name. Wesley also regarded the contempt shown toward the "holy club" as a mark of a true Christian.

Beyond the good works and outward piety, Wesley cultivated inner holiness. He developed a list of "general questions" in 1730. He further developed these questions into an elaborate grid, in which he recorded his daily activities hour-by-hour to determine if he had broken or kept his resolutions. He would then rank his hourly "temper of devotion" on a scale of one to nine.

JOURNEY TO SAVANNAH, GEORGIA

On October 14, 1735, Wesley and his brother Charles sailed to Savannah, Georgia. James Oglethorpe, who had founded a colony there, requested that Wesley become the minister of a newly formed Savannah parish.

On the voyage to the colonies, the Wesleys first came into contact with Moravians, who were also going to Georgia. Wesley was impressed by their faith and spirituality, deeply rooted in Pietism. At one point in the voyage, a storm arose and broke the mast off the ship. While the English panicked, the Moravians calmly sang hymns and prayed. This experience led Wesley to believe that the Moravians possessed an inner strength which he lacked. The deeply personal spirituality that the Moravians practiced heavily influenced Wesley's theology of Methodism.[10]

They reached Savannah on February 8, 1736, and Wesley began to spread Christianity to those in the colony. Wesley observed how the Moravians would break up into smaller bands and how instrumental they were in promoting holiness. Wesley copied their pattern in Georgia and divided the larger body of believers into smaller bands that he asked to meet weekly to exhort each other and to grow in the faith.[11]

Wesley's mission, however, faced constant challenges. He had developed a romantic relationship with Sophia Hopkey, a woman who had journeyed across the Atlantic on the same ship as Wesley. Wesley abruptly broke off the relationship on the advice of a Moravian minister in whom he confided. Hopkey contended that Wesley had promised to marry her and therefore had gone back on his word in breaking off the relationship. Wesley's problems came to a head when he refused Hopkey communion. She and her new husband, William Williamson, filed suit against Wesley.

Wesley stood trial and faced the accusations made by Hopkey. When the proceedings ended in a mistrial, Wesley felt his

---

10. Taken from article called, "Methodism," at http://en.wikipedia.org/wiki/Methodism. Accessed on Friday, December 20, 2013,

11. David Lowes Watson, p. 80.

reputation had already been tarnished too greatly, and he made it known that he intended to return to England.

Williamson raised charges against Wesley to prevent him from leaving the colony, but he managed to return to England. He left exhausted by the whole experience. His mission to Georgia contributed to a lifelong struggle with self-doubt. Wesley returned to England depressed and beaten. It was at this point that he turned to the Moravians. Both he and Charles received counsel from the young Moravian missionary, Peter Bohler, who was temporarily in England awaiting permission to depart for Georgia himself.

MORAVIAN INFLUENCE

On May 24, 1738 Wesley attended a Moravian meeting in Aldersgate Street, London. Wesley heard a reading of Martin Luther's preface to the Epistle to the Romans and penned the now famous lines, "I felt my heart strangely warmed." He wrote about that experience,

> I went very unwillingly to a Society in Aldersgate Street where one was reading about Luther's preface to The Epistle to the Romans. About a quarter before nine while he was describing the change which God works in the heart through faith in Christ, I felt my heart strangely warmed. I felt I did trust in Christ, Christ alone for salvation, and an assurance was given me that He had taken away my sins, even mine.

Wesley was led to the assurance of salvation and a deep personal relationship with God at that meeting. He was so impacted by God through the Moravians that he travelled to Germany to meet with Count Zinzendorf at Herrnhut,

> The Count received us in a manner I was quite unacquainted with, and therefore know not how to express. I believe his behavior was not unlike that of his Master (if we may compare human with divine) when he took the little children in his arms and blessed them. We should have been much amazed at him, but that we saw ourselves encompassed with a cloud of those who were all followers of him, as he is of Christ. Eighty-eight of them praise God with one heart and one mouth.[12]

Wesley, the keen observer, was taking meticulous notes while he met with the Count and studied their practices and methodology. He had an extraordinary ability to adapt principles and concepts to his own context. Latourette notes that he had "... an unusual capacity to accept suggestions and to adopt and adapt methods from various quarters."[13] He knew that what he saw in Herrnhut would not work in the same way in the urban centers of London. Henderson writes,

> At the settlement of Herrnhut, Wesley observed the Moravian community with great fascination. Following a custom he had practiced since his student days at Oxford, he spent much of time "collecting," or making terse observations and evaluations in a pocket notebook. His orderly mind reveled in their close administrative process, and for three weeks he scrutinized their entire plan of operation, taking copious and meticulous notes. Count Zinzendorf

---

12. George W. Forrell, *Nine Public Lectures on Important Subjects of Religion* (Iowa City, Iowa: University of Iowa Press), pp. xiii-xiv.

13. Latourette, p. 1,026.

> had arranged the community into compact cells, or "bands" as he called them, for spiritual oversight and community administration.[14]

Although Wesley was very positive about many practices he observed, he also critiqued others. He felt the Moravian groups were too withdrawn from the world and not engaging people enough. He also considered Count Zinzendorf too controlling and that the Moravians didn't have the freedom to do things apart from his watchful eye.[15] Wesley felt that those in the Moravian bands should minister to one another and not be controlled by a monitoring system. David Watson writes,

> In the Rules of Band-Societies which Wesley drew up for the Methodists in December of the same year, he stressed precisely the quality he felt was lacking in the Moravian system of monitors: mutual confession and accountability. The leader of the band, "some person among us," was to "speak his own state first, and then ask the rest, in order, as many and as searching questions as may be."[16]

Late in 1739 Wesley became more concerned with the Moravians and eventually broke off from them entirely, while maintaining his ties to the Anglican Church. He felt that some Moravians in London practiced the error of Quietism. They would ask people who doubted their faith to be still until faith

14. Henderson, p. 59.

15. David Lowes Watson, p. 82.

16. Ibid., p. 83.

arose.[17] He decided to form his own followers into a separate society. He then began the Methodist Society in England and started similar societies in Bristol, Kingswood, and throughout England.[18] Wesley followed principles and practices from the Moravians, but he also adapted and rejected other elements.

The Moravian Legacy to Wesley's Methodology	
Elements Wesley Liked	Elements Wesley Didn't Like
-Hymn singing as a form of instruction -Women's place of service -Special services: "Agape feast," "Watch nights" -Ecclesiolae in ecclesia -Intense fellowship: unity before information -Emphasis on conduct, no speculation -Emphasis on instantaneous conversion, assurance of salvation -Distinction of choirs for instruction and bands for edification	-Lack of openness, frankness, and simplicity of speech -Exclusiveness -Domination by Zinzendorf -Antinomianism -The Moravian doctrine of "stillness" -Downgrading the "means of grace," like communion and baptism -Making decisions by casting lots -A tendency toward mysticism -Subjective piety unrelated to human affairs

17. The actual philosophy called "Quietism" was a system of Christian mysticism that requires a withdrawal from the world, a renunciation of the individual will, and passive contemplation of God and divine things. It was condemned by the Roman Catholic Church in 1687 for wrongly elevating contemplation over meditation, intellectual stillness over vocal prayer, and interior passivity over pious action. This wasn't the official position of the Moravians, but Wesley felt that certain practices leaned toward Quietism. Of course, what worked well on the Zinzendorf's estate in Germany was very difficult to apply in the loud, bustling urban environment of London. The masses of England couldn't enjoy the seclusion and privilege of waiting like those under Zinzendorf. Ultimately, Wesley had to find his own way and develop his own style of small groups.

18. W. p. Stephens, "Wesley and the Moravians," *John Wesley: Contemporary Perspectives,* John Stacey, ed. (London: Epworth Press, 1988), p. 35.

The Methodism that Wesley eventually established drew from many sources and movements. George Hunter succinctly notes,

> He learned from exposure to the home groups (the ecclesiolae in ecclesia) that the Lutheran Pietist leader Philipp Jacob Spener developed to fuel renewal and outreach, and Wesley learned particularly from the Moravians. Wesley also learned from Anabaptist groups and from the occasional "societies" within the Church of England, so his group movement was eclectic Protestant.[19]

Wesley viewed his groups as a mix between the Pietisic Colegia of Spener and the religious societies of England. The members were supposed to pray together, receive words of exhortation, and to watch over each other. Another important role was to communicate the vital role of the Christian faith to the poor and those who were not able to read and learn.[20]

The movement that Wesley started was unique and thoroughly rooted in English society as a way to reform the Anglican Church and spread scriptural holiness throughout the land. Along with the small groups, Wesley employed the unconventional method of open-air preaching.

OPEN-AIR PREACHING

In February 1739, Wesley's Oxford friend, George Whitefield, began preaching in the open-air to a company of miners. Wesley hesitated to accept Whitefield's call to copy this bold step.

---

19. George G. Hunter III, *Church for the Unchurched* (Nashville, TN: Abingdon Press, 1996), p. 84.

20. Kenneth J. Collins, *John Wesley* (Nashville, Abingdon Press, 2003), p. 121.

Wesley thought that preaching in the open-air was very strange, but Whitefield set the example and Wesley followed.

Wesley realized that many would never enter a church building and open-air meetings gave people the opportunity to hear the gospel. Wesley preached wherever he could assemble people, even using his father's tombstone at Epworth as a pulpit. Wesley continued for fifty years—taking his stand in the fields, in halls, cottages, chapels, and even entering churches when he was invited.

Clergy attacked Wesley's open-air preaching in sermons and in print, and at times mobs attacked him. Wesley and his followers continued to work among the neglected and needy, although they were denounced as promoters of strange doctrines, fomenters of religious disturbances, blind fanatics, claiming miraculous gifts, attacking the clergy of the Church of England, and trying to re-establish Catholicism. Like the early Waldensians, early Methodism utilized open-air preaching effectively, but unlike the Waldensians, they were able to continue preaching in the open-air, in spite of the opposition.

Wesley felt that the Anglican Church failed to call sinners to repentance, that many of the clergy were corrupt, and that people were not hearing the gospel of salvation within the church buildings. He believed he was commissioned by God to bring about revival in the church, and no opposition, persecution, or obstacles could prevail against the divine urgency and authority of this commission.

Realizing that he and the few clergy helping him could not get the job done alone, as early as 1739, he began to approve local lay preachers. Members of the small groups (classes) wanted to preach in the open-air, and at first Wesley hesitated. Then his mother Susanna told him that by not letting them preach, he would be quenching the Holy Spirit. He yielded, and lay preachers became an important feature of Methodism.[21] He did evaluate each lay preacher and approved them, even though they were not ordained by the Anglican Church.

SPREADING HOLINESS

Wesley defined holiness as having one's heart fully fixed on God, setting aside all other affections. This emphasis on sanctification or holy living became the hallmark of Wesley's movement. He often said that the mission of Methodism was to "spread scriptural holiness throughout the land." Wesley claimed that a believer could reach Christian perfection or perfect love, when "all inward sin is taken away."[22] This was Wesley's most distinctive doctrine that was taaught throughout his lifetime.

Wesley's unique theology centered on the correlation of justification by faith with good works. Wesley's friend, Whitefield, a Calvinist, maintained that sin remains in the hearts of believers—thereby rejecting Wesley's notion of Christian perfection.[23] Whitefield considered Wesley naïve and overly optimistic to believe in Christian perfection.

Wesley and the Moravians also separated over the issue of holiness. The Moravians believed that a person's holiness came

---

21. Latourette, p. 1027.

22. *The Works of the Rev. John Wesley,* Vol. VI, 3rd edition, John Emory, ed., seven volumes, (New York: The Methodist Book Concern, 1825), p. 498.

23. Kenneth J. Collins, *John Wesley* (Nashville, Abingdon Press, 2003), p. 116.

from Christ alone, whereas the Wesleyans believed that one could achieve a state of Christian perfection (often called "perfect love") in this life. The Moravians followed the Lutheran teaching of total depravity.[24] Joseph Hutton writes,

> The more Wesley studied the writings of the Brethren the more convinced he became that in many ways they were dangerous teachers. . . . John Wesley held that the Brethren, like Molther, laid a one-sided stress on the doctrine of justification by faith alone. They were, he contended, Antinomians; they followed too closely the teaching of Luther; they despised the law, the commandments, good works, and all forms of self-denial.[25]

As an Anglican, Wesley affirmed the validity and authority of the visible church, but he was also influenced by the Puritan concept of the gathered church, based on Scripture alone. Wesley emphasized both concepts. He acknowledged the validity of a gathered community, elected by God for a purpose. But this did not negate the wider concept of an inclusive and visible church. Thus, Wesley never separated from the Anglican Church, but taught his followers to maintain their allegiance as Anglicans.[26]

FAREWELL

---

24. George W. Forrell, *Nine Public Lectures on Important Subjects of Religion* (Iowa City, Iowa: University of Iowa Press), pp. xvii-xix.

25. Joseph Edmund Hutton, Kindle Locations 3715-3720.

26. David Lowes Watson, p. 20.

Wesley died on March 2, 1791, in his eight-seventh year. As he lay dying, his friends gathered around him, and Wesley grasped their hands saying repeatedly, "Farewell, farewell." Then he said, "The best of all is, God is with us," lifted his arms and raised his feeble voice again, repeating the words, "The best of all is, God is with us." He was entombed at Wesley's Chapel, which he built in greater London. The site is now a place of worship and a visitor attraction, incorporating the Museum of Methodism and John Wesley's house.

Because he gave all to charity, Wesley died poor, leaving as the result of his life's work 153,000 members and 541 itinerant preachers. It has been said that when John Wesley was carried to the grave, he left behind him a good library of books, a well-worn clergyman's gown, and the Methodist Church.

LESSONS LEARNED

- John and Charles Wesley owed most of what they were and did to their mother's diligent training, high moral expectations, pious example, and hours of spiritual instruction.
- Wesley adapted ministry principles and then critiqued them to determine if they would fit a particular context and situation. For example, he learned a lot from the Moravians but also adapted their teachings to the bustling cities of England. He didn't accept everything from George Whitefield but did use Whitefield's unconventional preaching style.
- Wesley first learned about bands from the Moravians but also emphasized mutual accountability and less hierarchical control.
- Wesley promoted holiness and felt that small groups were the best way to help people grow in holiness.

Chapter 12

THE METHODISTS

John and Mary Smith participated in a class meeting that transformed their lives. They were poor factory workers who, like most, had heard about the class meetings by word of mouth. They received permission to attend two times before making a decision to join. They loved the free flow of ideas, transparent sharing, and most of all, they felt closer to God.

That night in May 1747, they attended the class meeting at George's home, who was also the leader. George opened the meeting with prayer. John and Mary, a newly married couple, felt comfortable with the wide mixture of singles and married couples. That night, like always, they passionately sang the two songs, and afterwards they knew exactly what George would ask: "How does your soul prosper?" They had been anticipating George's words all week. They shared honestly to the eleven people gathered in George's house. Mary said that she enjoyed her prayer time and was growing. John confessed that on two mornings he had rushed off to the factory without even opening his Bible. He asked the group to pray for him. Both needed prayer to be better witnesses at the local Bristol shirt factory. George moved on to others in the group and asked them the same question. He had a way of asking the question differently to make sure each person answered honestly and transparently.

Some squirmed and were less than transparent, but others confidently shared God's holy work in their lives. Everyone felt like they were part of something greater than themselves, a quest to spread holiness throughout the land. John and Mary felt they were part of an army that would cleanse England, convert lost souls, and change the nation.

THE PRIORITY OF SMALL GROUPS

Wesley viewed preaching as the preamble of what would take place in the small groups. Discipleship took place in the lay-led class meetings through mutual ministry. Henderson writes, "The class meeting was the most influential instructional unit in Methodism and probably Wesley's greatest contribution to the technology of group experience."[1] Although amazingly simple, it had a long-lasting impact that educators and religious leaders alike praised. A biography by Adam Clarke (who was a Methodist preacher during Wesley's lifetime) recounted Wesley's insistence about the priority of class meetings,

1. Henderson, p. 93.

> From long experience I know the propriety of Mr. Wesley's advice: "Establish class-meetings and form societies wherever you preach and have attentive hearers; for, wherever we have preached without doing so, the word has been like seed by the way-side" . . . Mr. Whitefield, when he separated from Mr. Wesley, did not follow it. What was the consequence? The fruit of Mr. Whitefield's labor died with himself. Mr. Wesley's remains and multiplies.[2]

The class meetings were Wesley's strategy for making disciples, rather than hearers of sermons. Henry Ward Beecher said, "The greatest thing John Wesley ever gave to the world is the Methodist class meeting." Dwight L. Moody, nineteenth-century revivalist, said, "The class-meetings are the best institutions for training converts the world ever saw."[3]

THE INTERLOCKING SYSTEM: BANDS, CLASSES, SOCIETIES

Wesley called his three interlocking groups *bands, classes,* and *societies.* In modern terms Wesley's groups are similar to accountability groups (bands), cells (classes), and large group worship (societies).

---

2. J. W. Etheridge, *The Life of the Rev. Adam Clarke* (New York: Carlton and Porter, 1859), 189, as quoted in Kevin Watson (2013-11-01), *The Class Meeting: Reclaiming a Forgotten (and Essential) Small Group Experience* (Kindle Location 1816). Asbury Seedbed Publishing. Kindle Edition.

3. As quoted in Henderson, p. 93.

BANDS

The bands were started in 1738, before the classes, and followed the Moravian pattern of promoting the spiritual renewal of each member.[4] The bands were organized according to sex, age, and marital status and usually had about six people.[5] They were homogeneous groups that met together for more intimate fellowship with the goal of transformation.[6] Unlike the classes, attendance was not required and only about twenty percent of those in the Methodist movement ever joined a band.[7]

In each band meeting, the members asked each other about the sins they had committed since the last meeting, the temptations they had to deal with, and how they were delivered from those temptations. The questions they would ask each other were:

- What known sins have you committed since the last meeting?
- What temptations have you met with?
- How were you delivered?
- What have you thought, said, or done which may or may not be sin?

---

4. Latourette, p. 1026.

5. Brown, p. 38.

6. These were not one-on-one discipleship meetings, a practice that later became very popular in America. Rather the bands prioritized smaller group interaction for the purpose of transformation. One-on-one interaction did exist between members and class leaders with his or her supervisor, but the band was a group experience.

7. Young, p. 112.

Because attendance was not required, the bands failed to multiply like the classes.[8] Doyle sums up the purpose of the bands,

> . . . these were small groups of around six members, men and women in separate groups, who met weekly for confession of sin and pastoral care. Only people assured of salvation could join and only those who desired a deeper, more intimate fellowship.[9]

The class meeting was the focal point among the Methodists, although the bands had their place and were important. Even as the classes became the basic unit of Methodist organization, the bands were not neglected.

CLASSES

After developing the bands and societies, Wesley was still frustrated with the lack of close pastoral oversight, especially for those who had been recently converted. The classes came into being as a way to make sure every member was held accountable. Actually, the initial classes developed for a different reason: to raise money.

In 1742, a group of Methodists were trying to figure out how to pay off a building debt in Bristol, England. Captain Foy suggested that the Bristol society be divided up into groups of twelve people. One person in each group would be designated the leader and would be responsible for visiting everyone in the group every week in order to collect one penny from each of them. By this means, Foy believed the building debt could be paid off. Someone expressed the concern that this would

8. Bunton, p. 64.

9. Young, p. 112.

prevent the poorest Methodists from being involved. Captain Foy responded by volunteering to take the eleven poorest members of the Bristol society into his group. He would visit them each week and ask them if they could contribute. If they were not able to do so, he would personally pay their pennies for them. Then, he challenged the other people at the meeting to do the same thing.

As this plan was put into practice, it became apparent that many Methodists were not keeping the "General Rules," which every Methodist was expected to keep. The General Rules were: do no harm, do good, and attend upon the ordinances of God.[10] Wesley realized that the class leaders could help help Methodists practice the General Rules and collect the weekly offering.[11] He also understood that the classes would help each person grow spiritually and care for one another.

The classes became a vital part of the Methodist movement and from 1742 onward, it was no longer possible to be a member of the larger society unless the person was part of a class.[12] Wesley summed up his attitude about the classes, saying, "Those who will not meet in a class cannot stay with us."[13] To put it another way, in Methodism, you weren't allowed to join the large group (society) before joining the small group (class).[14]

---

10. The "ordinances of God" referred to the Christian practices or spiritual disciplines (e.g., public worship, private prayer, Bible reading,and so forth).

11. Kevin Watson, Kindle Locations 377-390.

12. Bunton, p. 63.

13. Wesley, *Wesley's Works*, Vol. 2 (London, Wesleyan-Methodist Book-Room), p. 482.

14. Young, p. 113.

The class meetings were heterogeneous mixed groups in terms of sex, age, social standing, and spiritual readiness. Wesley visualized the class meeting as the point of entry for most initiates into Methodism, and he wanted the entry groups to be a warm fellowship of fellow strugglers, representing a cross-section of Methodism.[15] The size of most classes was five to twenty. One class member of that time period wrote, "A class-meeting, at present, consists of an indefinite number of persons, generally from twelve to twenty; though sometimes fewer even than twelve."[16]

SOCIETIES

The societies became the sum total of the classes and bands. To attend the society meeting, a person had to have a ticket that showed he or she was a faithful member of a class meeting. These tickets were the entrance permits to the society meetings. They were renewable quarterly and lack of attendance at class meetings excluded the person from entering the next quarter's society meetings. The goal was for the person who faltered in attendance to repent and turn more fully to Christ.[17]

The societies did not meet weekly, like the class meetings. Rather, they met each quarter, and the main focus was teaching God's Word and worshipping together. People who remained committed to Jesus and attended the class each week were automatically made part of the society after three months.[18] Hunter makes an important comparison,

---

15. Henderson, p. 98.

16. David Lowes Watson, p. 95.

17. Bunton, pp. 63-64.

18. Hunter III, p. 85.

> A Methodist Society was composed of the sum total of classes attached to it. As one's membership in early Christianity was primarily to a house church and somewhat secondarily to the whole church within the city, so in early Methodism one's primary membership was in the class and somewhat secondarily in the society.[19]

The society meetings were carefully scheduled to not conflict with any of the services of the Church of England.[20] Wesley wanted his movement to be submissive to the Anglican Church and covey the message, "we are loyal Anglicans and not in competition or opposition to the Church of England."[21] Throughout his life, Wesley remained within the established Anglican Church of England and insisted that his movement stay within Anglicanism.

Wesley didn't have to deal with major church polity issues because those were already established in the Church of England. He was more concerned about transforming those members who were part of the Anglican Church and reaching those without a relationship with Jesus. Some have compared the Wesley movement to a religious order, or a movement within a movement.

BACK TO PRIMITIVE CHRISTIANITY

Wesley desired to base everything he did on the Bible. Even though the classes started as a way to raise money, Wesley

---

19. Ibid., p. 85.

20. Henderson, p. 85.

21. Ibid., p. 85.

didn't want to continue them unless he could see their basis in Scripture. He wrote, "I could not but observe, this is the very thing which was from the beginning of Christianity. . . . The first preachers met in these catechumens, as they were called, apart from the great congregation, that they might instruct, rebuke, exhort, and pray with them, according to their several necessities."[22]

Wesley was a student of the primitive church and believed that the Church of England was a fallen church that needed revival. He wanted to help it come back to the primitive ideal.[23] He felt that long term transformation required an effective organizational structure, and he worked hard to build an extensive small group network. Hunter notes,

> Wesley also observed that certain normative behaviors were characteristic of life in the primitive church. They met together "to stir up one another to love and good works . . . encouraging one another" (Heb. 10:24-25). They seemed to have taught, admonished, exhorted, and prayed for one another. They rejoiced with those who rejoiced, and wept with those who wept (Rom. 12:15). Their behaviors toward one another ranged from telling one's sins to another (Matt. 18:15-18) to building one another up (1 Thess. 5:11). And Wesley believed the earliest churches followed the script of James (5:16): "Confess your sins to one another, and pray for one another, that you may be healed." With regret, Wesley did not see such behavior in his Anglican Church. One of the causes of this, he believed,

22. As quoted in Stanley Aysling, *John Wesley* (New York: Collins Publishers, 1979), p. 132.

23. Hunter III, pp. 124-125.

> was the lack of small groups, a deficiency not present in the early church's house churches.[24]

Wesley realized that as he drew people together in classes to challenge and encourage each other, the contagion and power of the apostolic church would move in human history once again.[25] He wrote,

> Never omit meeting your Class or Band; never absent yourself from any public meeting. These are the very sinews of our Society; and whatever weakens, or tends to weaken, our regard for these, or our exactness in attending them, strikes at the very root of our community.[26]

Weakening the class structure, according to Wesley, would strike at the root of Methodism. Like the early church, the Methodist groups mainly met in homes, but they also gathered in shops, schoolrooms, attics, even coal-bins—wherever there was room for ten or twelve people to assemble. Some pious followers would walk long distances, endure hardship, and put up with bizarre settings in order to attend their class.[27]

MAKING DISCIPLES

The class meeting was never an end in itself; rather it was a means to make disciples. Some wonder why more literature wasn't

---

24. Ibid., p. 125.

25. Ibid., p. 125.

26. John Wesley, "A Plain Account of Christian Perfection ," in *Works*, Jackson, 11: 433, as quoted in Kevin Watson, Kindle Locations 1828-1829.

27. Henderson, p. 99.

written about the Methodist class meetings during the time of Wesley. David Lowe Watson believes that those in Wesley's day were more concerned about why they were meeting and what they planned on accomplishing, rather than the specifics of the meeting itself.[28] They met to become stronger followers of Jesus, increase in holiness, and ultimately transform England. People were supposed to work out their salvation gradually over time and to develop in maturity. Conversions were just the first step in a gradual process of becoming like Jesus. Henderson writes,

> One of the key elements of the class meeting was the willingness to confront sin and be real about each member's dark past. They weren't to hide anything. One of the remarkable features of the class meeting format was the realism about human nature that was built into its design.[29]

Meeting weekly helped them to sustain the discipleship process and maintain accountability. David Watson says, "The genius of Wesley's organization of the Methodist societies lay in his recognition that Christian discipleship was first and foremost a response to God's grace."[30] The classes weren't as intense as the bands; nor were they designed for intensive counseling sessions or in-depth Bible studies. The dynamic of Christian fellowship quickly developed, as members began to "bear one another's burdens," and to "care for each other." Wesley writes,

28. David Lowes Watson, p. xi.

29. Henderson, p. 103.

30. David Lowes Watson, p. 87

> Many now happily experienced that Christian fellowship of which they had not so much as an idea before. They began to "bear one another's burdens," and "naturally" to "care for each other." As they had daily a more intimate acquaintance with, so they had a more endeared affection for each other. And "speaking the truth in love, they grew up into Him in all things which is the head, even Christ; from whom the whole body, fitly joined together, and compacted by that which every joint supplied, according to the effectual working in the measure of every part, increased unto the edifying itself in love."[31]

The only requirement for joining a class meeting was the desire to flee from the wrath to come. A person needed to be willing to grow in holiness and take the steps necessary to separate from sin and separate to God. Hunter writes, "In time, two years on the average, most members experienced justification and new birth; and from that point on they 'expected' to experience 'sanctification,' that is, 'being made perfect in love' in this life."[32]

The early Methodists would boldly reduce the number of people if any sin was noticed. They wanted a pure society, free from the contamination of sin. In fact, guests were only allowed to visit a class on a trial basis. The visitor needed to understand the rules of the society and make a commitment to those rules. There were many instances of tickets being refused each quarter to those who failed to abide by them.[33] And the quarterly renewal

31. As quoted in Kevin Watson, Kindle Location 1823.

32. Hunter III, p. 121.

33. David Lowes Watson, p. 108.

of class tickets became not only a disciplinary examination, but also an occasion when all of the members, including the leader, were questioned about their spiritual growth.[34] The class meeting functioned to determine whether a Methodist was walking in the grace of God, and through the class meetings, Wesley pruned the Methodist vine.[35]

More than anything, the class meeting was the chief way to keep the newly converted from slipping back into their former way of life. Wesley wrote,

> I am more and more convinced, that the devil himself desires nothing more than this, that the people of any place should be half-awakened, and then left to themselves to fall asleep again. Therefore I determine, by the grace of God, not to strike one stroke in any place where I cannot follow the blow.[36]

Unlike that of the more general society, the purpose of the Methodist class was chiefly one of discipline, to discern, as Wesley put it, "whether they [were] indeed working out their own salvation."[37] Wesley was convinced that people rarely made progress in holiness by themselves. Wesley explicitly criticized George Whitefield's inattention to the class meeting in Pembrokeshire in his published journal in 1763,

---

34. Ibid., p. 110.

35. Kenneth J. Collins, *John Wesley* (Nashville, Abingdon Press, 2003), p. 122.

36. Wesley, March 13, 1743, "Journals and Diaries II" (1738-1743), Vol. 19 in *Works*, 318.

37. Collins, p. 122.

> I was more convinced than ever that the preaching like an apostle, without joining together those that are awakened and training them up in the ways of God, is only begetting children for the murderer. How much preaching has there been for these twenty years all over Pembrokeshire! But no regular societies, no discipline, no order or connection. And the consequence is that nine in ten of the once awakened are now faster asleep than ever.[38]

Without the small group structure, Wesley felt that preaching brought forth little lasting fruit. In fact, both George Whitefield and John Wesley preached continually in the open-air. Many were saved under Whitefield and Wesley. Both had similar histories and were excellent in open-air preaching. Both witnessed thousands of conversions through their ministries. Benjamin Franklin once calculated that Whitefield could easily preach to a crowd of thirty thousand people—without a microphone. Whitefield probably even recorded more decisions than Wesley because of the huge crowds he attracted.

Yet, there were some major differences between the two as well. At the end of his life George Whitefield said this: "My brother Wesley acted wisely—the souls that were awakened under his ministry he joined in classes, and thus preserved the fruits of his labor. This I neglected, and my people are a rope of sand."[39] Wesley organized the movement and brought it under systematic management; Whitefield hoped that those who had been "awakened" would follow through on their initiative; Wesley left nothing to chance.

---

38. Wesley, "Journal for August 25, 1763," in *Works*, 21: 424, as quoted in Kevin Watson, Kindle Location 1856.

39. Henderson, p. 30.

REPORTING ON YOUR SOUL

The class meeting was not a highly organized event. It normally lasted for one hour, and the main focus was "reporting on your soul."[40] The class would begin with an opening song or two. Then the leader would share a personal, religious experience. Afterwards, he would inquire about the spiritual life of those in the group. Each member would give a testimony about his or her spiritual condition. After participants answered the question, the leader would turn to someone else in the group and ask the same question.

The class leader or someone else would respond to the person's answer by offering encouragement, and sometimes giving advice. Then other members would share about their spiritual lives. The basic pattern of the meeting was that simple. People were essentially giving testimony to their experience of God over the past week. And God used this format to transform lives and hold each person accountable to live a holy life. People often experienced conversion simply through participating in a class meeting![41] Before closing in prayer, there would be an offering to support the ministry. Mallison writes, "Every member was expected to belong, to speak freely and plainly about every subject from their own temptations to plans for establishing a new cottage meeting or visiting the distressed."[42]

---

40. Snyder, p. 55.

41. Thomas R. Albin, "'Inwardly Persuaded': Religion of the Heart in Early British Methodism," in *Heart Religion" in the Methodist Tradition and Related Movements*, Richard B. Steele, ed. (Lanham, MD: Scarecrow Press, 2001), 45, as quoted in Kevin Watson, Kindle Locations 1826-1827.

42. John Mallison, *Growing Christians in Small Groups* (London: Scripture Union, 1989), pp. 127-128.

It might be hard to understand what the class meeting would look like today, or why it had such a powerful impact back then. Hunter explains,

> But because eighteenth-century Methodism's experience took place in a different time and culture from our own, the deeper meaning or mission of the class meetings is not so obvious today, and at least several scholars have tried to pinpoint it. Gloster's Udy's pioneering scholarship (1962) concluded that the primary mission of the class meetings was to provide people with the kind of family experience that the upheaval and fragmenting of the industrial revolution had robbed from them. The class experiences inculcated interpersonal values and facilitated people's growth and development.[43]

Wesley would often use the "one-anothers," such as bearing each other's burden, to describe the essence of the class meetings. They were a family away from family, just like the early house churches. What took place in the early Methodist class meetings resembles what the writer of Hebrews says,

> See to it, brothers, that none of you has a sinful, unbelieving heart that turns away from the living God. But encourage one another daily, as long as it is called Today, so that none of you may be hardened by sin's deceitfulness (3:12-13).

One way the members ministered to God and one another was through hymn singing. One member of a class back in Wesley's

43. Hunter III, p. 121.

day talked about singing being an important part of the class meeting. He writes,

> As singing forms a considerable portion of the service at a class meeting, I must give you one or two specimens of their hymns . . . They are poured forth in the most soft, soothing, languishing, and melting strains that music is capable of; and music, you know, has charms to soothe a savage beast.[44]

EVANGELISM AND MULTIPLICATION

As mentioned earlier, Wesley was not convinced that a person had made a decision for Christ until he was involved in a small group. In fact, it was often in the small group that people were born again. Young writes, "The classes served as an evangelistic tool and as a discipling agent."[45] Even if people accepted Jesus during the field preaching, they would work out what that meant in the class meetings. The classes would nurture the person's response and help him or her make it real. Brown says,

> The groups also had a clear evangelistic function as people were converted during the meetings and lapsed members were enabled to renew their commitment to Christ. Wesley knew that the beginnings of faith in a person's life could be incubated into saving faith more effectively in a warm Christian environment than it could in the chill of the world.[46]

---

44. David Lowes Watson, p. 97.

45. Young, p. 113.

46. Brown, p. 39.

Hunter talks about Wesley being "driven to multiply 'classes' for these served best as recruiting groups, as ports of entry for new people, and for involving awakened people with the gospel and power."[47] He knew that he needed a lot more classes to reach a lost world for Jesus. There was a constant sense of urgency and vision to reach people without Jesus.

When a class became too large, it would multiply to allow more room for others. However, one of the most common ways of starting new groups was through cell planting. Leaders were developed and then one or two would start the new groups and begin inviting the newly awakened souls.[48] T. A. Hegre writes,

> I believe that the success of Wesley was due to his habit of establishing small groups. His converts would meet regularly in groups of about a dozen people. If the group became too large, it would divide, and it might continue to divide again and again.[49]

Wesley would not start a class, if he could not effectively manage it, and he would not preach where he could not enroll people into classes.[50] Hunter notes, "He [Wesley] saw no virtue in starting new ministry or group life that dies soon after birth,

47. Hunter III, p. 56.

48. William Walter Dean, in his dissertation on the Wesley class system writes, "Cell division was much less common than might have been expected. The formation of new classes was by far the most frequent approach to growth" (Dean 1985:266).

49. Hegre, p. 8.

50. Hunter III, p. 56.

or is stunted in growth."[51] Wesley understood that discipleship was more important than simply getting a lot of people converted. Much of Wesley's strategy could be summarized in four maxims:

- Preach and visit in as many places as you can.
- Go most where they want you most.
- Start as many classes as can be effectively managed.
- Do not preach where you cannot enroll awakened people in classes.[52]

CLASS LEADERSHIP

The bands were more informal and didn't need a set leader. This wasn't true in the classes. Class leaders were the spiritual pastors who cared for those in the group. The leader kept track of attendance and visited people who missed the weekly meeting. In fact, one key reason for the success of the classes was the system of leadership. Wesley established certain principles for leadership:

- The leaders were appointed (as opposed to the bands where the leaders were elected).[53]
- Women were permitted to be lay leaders (they eventually became a majority).[54]Selection of leadership was based on moral and spiritual character, as well as common sense.[55]

51. David Lowes Watson, p. 119.

52. Hunter III, p. 56.

53. Pallil, p. 110.

54. Brown, p. 39.

55. Ibid.

- Leadership was "plural," that is, there was more than one leader, so that leadership was shared.[56] Snyder writes, "This was the normal system, based in part on Wesley's conviction that spiritual oversight had to be intimate and personal and that plural leadership was the norm in a congregation."[57]
- The class leaders were viewed as pastors.

Class leaders were called by different names such as *sub-pastors, non-commissioned officers*, and even *spiritual police*. What Wesley looked for in a leader was discipline, spirituality, and the commitment to help others become disciples of Jesus.[58] The class leader needed to keep his or her spiritual life vibrant, as we can see by Francis Asbury's description of a spiritual class leader in the 1798 *Doctrines and Discipline*,

> We have almost constantly observed, that when a leader is dull or careless or inactive—when he has not abilities or zeal sufficient to reprove with courage though with gentleness, and to press a present salvation upon the hearts of the sincere, the class is, in general, languid; but, on the contrary, when the leader is much alive to God and faithful in his office, the class is also, in general, lively and spiritual.[59]

---

56. Young, p. 113.

57. Snyder, p. 58.

58. David Lowes Watson, p. 101.

59. Frederick A. Norwood, ed., *The Doctrines and Discipline of the Methodist Episcopal Church in America.* With Explanatory Notes by Thomas Coke and Francis Asbury, Facsimile ed. (Evanston, IL : The Institute for the Study of Methodism and Related Movements, Garrett-Evangelical Theological

The class leaders had two key responsibilities:

1. To see each person in his class once a week in order to inquire how their souls prosper; to advise, reprove, comfort, or exhort, as occasion may require; to receive what they are willing to give toward the relief of the poor. In the Methodist rules, it says, "If possible, the Leader should see every one of his members once every week, and if in consequence of affliction or neglect, any member is absent from his class, that member should be without delay visited."[60]
2. To meet the minister and supervisors of the small groups (called stewards of the society) once a week; in order to inform the minister of any that are sick, or of any that walk disorderly, and will not be reproved; to pay to the stewards what they have received of their several classes in the week preceding; and to show their account of what each person has contributed.[61]

Getting people to attend the class meeting became more and more difficult as time went on. The following was taken from *The Wesley Banner and Revival* (written in 1849) at a time when Methodism had become more institutionalized,

> He [the leader] should urge his members to a weekly attendance upon their class, insisting, in spite of the excuses which some make for their irregular

---

Seminary, 1979), 147 (henceforth, 1798 *Doctrines and Discipline*), as quoted in Kevin Watson, Kindle Locations 1798-1801.

60. David Lowes Watson, p. 103.

61. David Lowes Watson, p. 98.

> attendance, that, generally, where there is a will, there is a way.[62]

To become a class leader, no formal training was necessary. The training was their experience. Henderson writes,

> The early Methodists believed that leadership was a quality which occurred naturally among groups of people and could not be produced as such, only recognized. Although training schools for ministers were frequently discussed, there was never any seminary or Bible school for Methodist leaders for well over one hundred years. In fact, there was no formal training program at all during the eighteenth century for them. No academic course "qualified" preachers or would-be-preachers for Methodist appointments. Rather local people who showed leadership ability were promoted upwards through a succession of minor offices until that ability was recognized at the upper levels by consecration to the itinerancy.[63]

Eventually the leaders began meeting on a weekly basis with their supervisors or "stewards," to receive encouragement and instruction.

SUPERVISION

Wesley was the chief visionary and promoter of the Methodist class meetings. Yet, Wesley had to keep stepping back and delegating to others at increasingly higher levels of leadership. Latourette says,

62. Ibid., p. 103.

63. Henderson, p. 149.

> For a time Wesley himself visited each of the societies to supervise them and enforce discipline. As they increased this became impossible and he assembled his preachers in annual conferences. . . . As societies and preachers further grew in numbers, he established "circuits" with traveling preachers and soon, as an assistant to himself, a superintendent was placed in charge of each circuit. He himself kept an autocratic control of the whole.[64]

Wesley tried his best to minister up-close and stay connected with the thriving ministry, but ultimately he realized he couldn't be present everywhere. He backed off and allowed others to take charge. The primary administrative oversight took place at the weekly supervisory meetings (society leadership). These supervisors were appointed by Wesley and would receive the reports of the leaders and offer counsel and encouragement. Henderson writes,

> Every Methodist was under someone else's direct and immediate supervision. There was a constant emphasis on "bearing one another's burdens," so that not even the slightest affliction went unnoticed. . . . The group processes of Methodism were under a simple but thorough system of constant surveillance. Just as a scientist can monitor a complicated and vast system by watching a panel or gauges, dials, and meters, so that Methodist local preacher could monitor the society by examining the class books and records that were regularly submitted.[65]

---

64. Latourette, p. 1,027.

65. Henderson, p. 144.

Supervising those who would pastor the flock was a critical reason why the Methodists were able to continue to grow. They cared for leaders on every level. The classes made up a society; the societies were organized by districts; and the districts were arranged by provinces or nations, with Wesley, the principal leader and visionary.

CLASS MEETINGS IN NORTH AMERICA

As Methodism was transplanted from British to American soil in the second half of the eighteenth century, the class meeting became firmly rooted in the American context. In fact, when Methodism became a formal denomination in the United States in 1784, the class meeting was listed as a requirement for membership. The early Methodists in North America removed those who didn't regularly attend a class meeting. They also used the ticket system as an entry checking method for the larger gathering. Yet those tickets gradually became more of a symbol of Methodist identity and were not a means of entry into the worship service.[66] Peter Cartwright was a nineteenth century Methodist preacher and politician in Illinois, who ran against Abraham Lincoln for a seat in the U.S. Congress in 1846, and lost. He wrote about the class,

> Class-meetings have been owned and blessed of God in the Methodist Episcopal Church, and from more than fifty years' experience, I doubt whether any one means of grace has proved as successful in building up the Methodist Church as this blessed privilege. . . . May the time never come when class-meetings shall be laid aside in the Methodist Episcopal Church, or when these class-meetings shall cease to be a test of

---

66. Kevin Watson, Kindle Locations 459-463.

> membership among us. I beg and beseech class-leaders to be punctual in attending their classes, and if any of their members stay away from any cause, hunt them up, find out the cause of their absence, pray with them and urge them to the all-important duty of regularly attending the class-meeting. Much, very much, depends on faithful and religious class-leaders; and how will the unfaithful class-leader stand in the judgment of the great day, when by his neglect many of his members will have backslidden, and will be finally lost?[67]

The class meetings gave men and women a sense of purpose and direction as they grew together in Christian holiness.

DECLINE OF CLASS MEETINGS

Many Methodists today have never even heard of a class meeting, and the majority are not practicing the weekly class meetings. The question is why?

FROM SOCIETY TO CHURCH

Wesley resisted separating from the Church of England to his dying day. This made the transition from society to church difficult after his death. Wesley argued that God had raised them up within the Church of England to be a "witnessing order." Because he refused to identify Methodism as a church, he was not forced to integrate the class structure within an independent local church. Watson writes, "Not only was this progression from society to church contrary to Wesley's reforming

---

67. Peter Cartwright, *The Autobiography of Peter Cartwright* (New York: Carlton and Porter, 1857), 519-520. Accessed at http://vitalpiety.com/author/deeplycommitted/page/5/ on Monday, December 23, 2013.

intentions: it proved to be debilitating for the class meeting."[68] Because Wesley didn't lead the change from society to church, the class structure became less important in the transition.

MEMBERSHIP

Wesley and others were quick to remove erring members in order to purify the society, but those same members could continue to participate in the Anglican Church, of which the Methodist Movement was a part. When Methodism ceased to be a voluntary society, removing someone from membership for failure to attend a class meeting became an issue. If a person was expelled from membership because of not attending a class meeting, it meant that the individual was excommunicated from the local church, cut off from the community of the faithful, and unable to participate in the sacraments.

Such a penalty seemed unduly harsh, especially for those who came regularly to the other meetings of the church. In 1889, the conference committee declared that the class was important but failure to join a class didn't cause a person to lose membership. The class became optional. It became another alternative for growth, but not the basis for joining the church. Watson writes,

> Given the lack of any clear Methodist doctrine of the church, the class meeting became a central means of fellowship rather than the basis of church membership, and the Wesleyan standards of personal holiness became more broadly social.[69]

---

68. David Lowes Watson, p. 136.

69. Ibid., p. 137.

THE NATURE OF THE CHURCH

We've seen that Methodism operated within the Anglican Church, and Wesley's passion was to reform the Anglican Church through the spread of scriptural holiness. Wesley never concerned himself with church structure and polity because all those in the Methodist movement were considered Anglicans. Wesley viewed the class meeting as one of the spiritual disciplines to become like Jesus. But he never considered the class as *the church.*

Involvement in a class was a means of grace, but since there was no clear doctrine of the church, class involvement was just one means of grace, among others. Henry Rack writes, "It [the class meeting] was always liable to suffer from other popular and perhaps less 'official' means of grace."[70] Wesley was quick to admit that his rules for the societies were merely human applications of divine rules. When Methodists came to regard themselves as an official church, they did not see the class as equally important as the larger church gathering on Sunday.

THE PROBLEM OF PRIORITIES

Methodist churches soon began to construct and own their buildings. Sunday school, programs, educational ministry, and other activities began to fill the church schedule. Many churches still believed in the class meeting, but it became less of a priority to insist that each member attend a weekly class meeting outside the building. Gradually, the need lessened to meet in home groups because of a new, modern structure and system

70. Henry Rack, "The Decline of the Class-Meeting and the Problems of Church-Membership in Nineteenth-Century Wesleyanism," WHS *Proc 39* (1973-1974), pp. 12-21.

of church life. After all, the church members were coming to hear the sermon each Sunday, attend Sunday school classes, and maybe a midweek prayer meeting. Perhaps some viewed the Sunday school as their class meeting or substituted their class meeting for the mid-week Bible study or prayer meeting within the church building. The center of church life, in other words, became focused on the activities in the building. A wide array of programs, meetings, and larger events eventually replaced the central place of the class meeting.

Charles Edward White noticed that the class meetings declined in America due to what he referred to as the *settled pastor*. He noticed that when there were circuit preachers, the class meeting was the center of church life because the pastor or circuit preacher would only visit occasionally and in his or her absence, the class functioned as the church. After pastors were appointed to the churches, there didn't seem to be the same need for class meetings. The sermon was sufficient.[71] Frederick Norwood observes:

> The high point of the class meeting coincides with the heyday of the circuit rider. Its decline dates from his dismounting. [Previously] the class leader was needed to perform those pastoral functions which are part of a balanced ministry. But when the preacher settled down . . . the class leader . . . became an unnecessary wheel.[72]

---

71. Charles Edward White, *The Rise and Decline of the Class Meeting* (Spring Arbor, Michigan). Accessed at http://myweb.arbor.edu/cwhite/cm.pdf on Monday, May 5, 2014.

72. Frederick A. Norwood, *The Story of American Methodism* (Nashville: Abingdon, 1974), p. 132.

When the "settled" pastor began to concern him or herself with all the structures and programs, it was often overwhelming to also prioritize the class meeting. Many began to view the class meeting as one more program. Some simply stopped fighting the tension between the larger gathering and the small cell. Watson writes,

> Confronted by the radical discipleship of these contemporary ecclesiola, there are many members of mainline North American churches who are only too aware of being challenged by a call to further commitment, but in all sincerity do not know how to answer it without rejecting most of what they have hitherto known as churchly activity. To become ecclesiola seems to present an unavoidable alienation from the ecclesia, however much a structural relationship is sought and maintained. It is not too much to say that for some, the tension of this dilemma is sufficiently intense for them to opt out of the struggle, and to settle for the blandness of folk religiosity.[73]

Many pastors replaced the transformational weekly class meetings with occasional small groups or task groups that were more like church programs than Wesleyan class meetings. Even the prayer meeting was a substitute for the class meeting, rather than a means to enhance it. During the 1830s, there were fewer and fewer references to the class meeting and this was about the time that churches began to emphasize church prayer meetings. Watson writes,

> During the 1830s, the role they [class meetings] had hitherto served as a door into the societies was

73. David Lowes Watson, p. 142.

> taken over by the prayer meeting—especially the after-preaching prayer meeting at the Communion rail or in the vestry. Indeed, spiritual vitality in general became more frequently related to prayer meetings than to classes. They were less structured and more spontaneous gatherings, and were more readily adaptable to the institutional activities of the chapel than the interpersonal spirituality of the class meetings. [74]

FROM TRANSFORMATION TO INFORMATION

Another reason for the decline of the class meeting was the change of emphasis from transformation to curriculum based learning groups. Kevin Watson wrote a 2013 book called *The Class Meeting: Reclaiming a Forgotten (and Essential) Small Group Experience*. He writes,

> The decline of the class meeting began in the mid-nineteenth century. The move away from the class meeting could be discussed in a variety of ways. One explanation is that the rise of the Sunday school movement gradually pushed the class meeting to the margins of Methodism, ultimately causing it to disappear altogether . . . the Sunday school movement led to an approach to small groups where a group of people gathered to learn from a perceived expert, either the leader of the small group or the author of a book the group was studying. In other words, the Sunday school movement shifted attention away from the focus on Christian experience and on becoming

74. Ibid., p. 137.

> a deeply committed Christian, which Asbury had so strongly endorsed.[75]

In early Methodism, personal growth in holiness was all important. As information became the new dominant priority, Sunday school became a growing phenomenon. People wanted to learn new truth but didn't feel the same need to meet in homes to talk about the state of their souls. In the early days, the class meeting was more about one's current relationship with God and how they were living it out. Yet as curriculum-driven groups became more important, those in the small groups assumed a learner's role—those who received information, rather than the role of an active participant.[76]

When a person is uncomfortable in talking about his or her relationship with God, a curriculum driven study can be less intimidating. A person can talk about content instead of really talking about a relationship with his or her creator. In many Methodist churches, the Methodist "classes" literally became Sunday school "classes."

Unfortunately, by the beginning of the twentieth century, the class meeting was almost entirely extinct in America. It was occasionally referred to by historians, but it was far easier to find an early Methodist class meeting ticket than a group of Methodists who were actually meeting together as a class meeting. Instead of talking to each other about their experience of God and their pursuit of holiness, Methodists were talking to each other about abstract ideas that were increasingly difficult to connect to the intimate and mundane details of their lives.

---

75. Kevin Watson, Kindle Locations 193-195.

76. Ibid., Kindle Locations 227-241.

The class meeting became an archaeological relic instead of the vehicle for Christian discipleship.[77]

LESSONS LEARNED

- The Wesleyan classes prioritized transparency and "plain speaking." The emphasis was transformation, rather than information.
- Participation in the classes was vital. Wesley knew that people had to experience ministry to grow.
- Wesley developed his future leaders from those who regularly attended classes, manifested godly character, and showed promising signs of leadership.
- Every leader in the Methodist system was closely supervised by a higher level leader.
- In the historical process of moving from volunteer society to Methodist denomination, the class meeting lost its priority. Wesley's voluntary society structure alongside the Anglican Church did not transfer well to the Methodist local church structure. Wesley was not able to guide the transition since he insisted on Methodism staying within the Anglican Church to his dying day
- Because Wesley was very careful not to establish another church that competed with the Anglican Church, he never developed the idea that the class was the church, comparable to a New Testament house church.

77. Ibid., Kindle Locations 802-808).

Chapter 13

MODERN HOUSE CHURCHES

From 1895 to 1903, Roland Allen served as an Anglican missionary to China. Thereafter, for the next forty years, he wrote about missionary principles that would not receive much public recognition until after his passing. He served as a forbearer and a prophet to the house church movements that have spread throughout the world. His most significant writings are captured in two books, *Missionary Methods: St. Paul's or Ours?* and *The Spontaneous Expansion of the Church.*

In contrast to the popular missionary methods of his day, where western missionaries imported western church models that depended upon western church leaders and western resources, he challenged the status quo making two primary observations,

1. We have allowed racial and religious pride to direct our attitude towards those whom we have been wont to call 'poor heathen.' We have approached them as superior beings, moved by charity to import of our wealth to destitute and perishing souls."[1]
2. "Want of faith has made us fear and distrust native independence. We have imagined ourselves to be, and we have acted so as to become, indispensable.[2]

The common missionary methods depended upon white men on a ministerial salary to run the mission organizations and establish churches. And the results were staggeringly low. Allen sought alternative ways to be the church on the mission field. He wanted to see the development of churches that were indigenous to the point that it depended upon the people of the native country and empowered them to minister without having to be paid. He wrote,

> We ought never to send a mission agent to do what men on the spot are already doing spontaneously. . . . If the moment we find anyone doing anything spontaneously we send a paid man to do it for him, we stop his work and we check others from following his example.[3]

---

1. Roland Allen, *Missionary Methods: St. Paul's or Ours?* (Grand Rapids: Eerdmans, 1962), p. 142.

2. Ibid., p. 143.

3. Allen, p. 38.

This meant that western leaders would have to give up the control of what they were producing. Allen wrote, "By spontaneous expansion I mean something which we cannot control."[4] More specifically he describes it this way:

> I mean the expansion which follows the unexhorted and unorganized activity of individual members of the church explaining to others the Gospel which they have found for themselves; I mean the expansion which follows the irresistible attraction of the Christian church for men who see its ordered life, and are drawn to it by desire to discover the secret of a life which they instinctively desire to share; I mean also the expansion of the church by the addition of new churches.[5]

The difference for Allen is that these churches would be "simple," native to the culture, and follow the pattern of meeting as found in the writings of Paul which describe the early church. They would not be dependent upon the trappings of western organizational oversight, but upon the fact that the Spirit is at work in God's people, whether or not it fits the expectations of western church leaders.

In his day, Allen's writings were met with little response on the mission field. However, historical circumstances of the twentieth century have proven that his words were prophetic beyond his expectations. From 1950 on, the global house church movement has resulted in a spontaneous multiplication of churches that has proven to be one of the most significant influences of the modern-day church.

---

4. Ibid., p. 13.

5. Ibid., p. 7.

Not only are small groups crucial to this kind of church, the small group is the church. The house church phenomenon has primarily taken on two manifestations. First, there is the independent house church. The second is shaped by a network mindset. Larry Kreider writes, "They are called house churches because each one functions as a little church. They are networks because they work together to foster accountability and encouragement."[6] Often they have been called church planting movements, but they are also referred to as organic churches or simple churches. The following brief survey will focus on the latter because the impact of house church networks outweighs that of independent house churches in significant ways. While there are many examples of house church networks that have arisen in the twentieth century, what follows will highlight four of the most significant.[7]

The sheer numbers of people who have met in house churches around the world are staggering. While it is quite difficult to ascertain exact data for the house church movements because of the underground nature of some and because most of these churches have been gathering in countries where the Christian church is persecuted or poor, we can examine a few movements to illustrate how house church networks operate.

HOUSE CHURCHES IN CHINA

The most significant example is found in China. David Garrison is one of the primary observers of what he calls *church planting movements.* He reports about China that in 1982 there

6. Larry Kreider, *House Church Networks* (Ephrata, PA: House to House Publications, 2001), p. 7.

7. For more on case studies see Rad Zdero, ed,, *Nexus: The World House Church Movement Reader* (Pasadena, CA: William Carey Library, 2007).

were about 1.3 million Christians, while eighteen years later this number had risen to nearly ninety million. All of this remarkable growth occurred in underground churches that met in homes after western missionaries were expelled from China following the Communist Revolution in 1949.[8]

When Mao Zedong announced the People's Republic of China on October 1, 1949, there were only about one million Protestant Christians in a country of over five hundred million people. At first, the new government allowed Christians to continue on as they were. However in the early 1950s, that all changed. An extensive persecution was unleashed. Hundreds of church leaders were imprisoned and sent to labor camps. In his book, *The Heavenly Man*, Brother Yun writes,

> In just one city in China, Wenzhou in Zhenjiang Province, 49 pastors were sent to prison labor camps near the Russian border in 1950. Many were given sentences of up to 20 years for their "crimes" of preaching the gospel. Of those 49 pastors just one returned home. Forty-eight died in prison. In my home areas of Nanyang believers were crucified on the walls of their churches for not denying Christ. Others were chained to vehicles and horses and dragged to their death.[9]

All of the external trappings of church life were destroyed. Church buildings and property were confiscated and either destroyed or re-purposed. Bibles and Christian education literature was burned. While many fell away from the faith in the midst of the fires of persecution, those who were left

---

8. David Garrison, *Church Planting Movements* (Arkadelphia, AR: Wigtake Resources, 2004), p. 52.

9. Brother Yun, *The Heavenly Man* (Grand Rapids: Kregel, 2002), p. 20.

were fully committed. In this setting, the church of China was forced to live out the principles that Roland Allen found in the Scriptures. They did not do so because of any theology or any equipping provided by missionaries. They did it out of shear necessity. One Chinese Christian writes of his experience during this time,

> Yes, we regard our meetings at home as a local church in spiritual fellowship with the worldwide Christian community. We began as a prayer group for Christian students at the University about 1952 when it had become untenable to have our meetings on campus ground. . . . So we met in my quarters in the professors' compound at four every Wednesday afternoon. We did the things we had always done in varsity fellowship—singing, Bible studies, intercession, fellowship, but with, I believe more depth and more personal openness . . .
>
> Between 1952 and 1964, the prayer group had its ups and downs. We never had more than thirty or more students. In 1962, there was only my wife and me. But the important thing was that God had left a Christian witness on campus . . .
>
> Unknowingly, our group turned itself into a church. By 1964 our church had about thirty people worshiping on Wednesdays. Only seven were students or members of the faculty. Others came from the neighborhood. We had a weekly communion service. . . .
>
> The years of the Cultural Revolution were a blank so far as our home meeting was concerned. I was assigned to work in a fruit-preserving factory. My wife

> went to live with her parents. There was not much to do. . . . Now I am back teaching physics and I have also got back to my quarters. We have resumed our house worship, but of the twenty we had before the time of the Red Guards, only eight are still around. However more new people have joined us. . . .
>
> I am in two minds about our future. On the one hand I would love a pastor to come to us, have a small church near the University and do good evangelism work. On the other hand, I can't help feeling that, given our peculiar situations, it might be best for us to continue to meet in homes, away from the limelight, quietly refracting the light of the Lord.[10]

Western missionaries of the time assumed that the church in China would die on the vine. One expelled missionary wrote,

> When all missionaries left China, the West was sometimes guilty of unbelieving pessimism. Seeing a weak and divided church, we felt we had failed. We knew many dedicated men and women and outstanding spiritual leaders. But could they, a tiny minority, stand against the tide of a triumphant communist ideology that proclaimed the 'Kingdom of man'—with no place for a crucified Savior?[11]

---

10. Raymond Fung, *Households of God on China's Soil* (Geneva: World Council of Churches Publications, 1982), 24-28, quoted in Robert and Julia Banks, *The Church Comes Home* (Peabody, MA: Hendrickson Publishers, 1998), pp. 62-63.

11. David H. Adeney, *China: The Church's Long March* (Ventura, CA: Regal Books, 1985), p. 206.

Imprisoned Chinese pastors thought much the same way. After their release in the 1970s, they returned home wondering what would be left of their churches. When they reached home, they found that not only had people been praying for them all those years, but their church fellowships had grown three, five, or ten times as large as before their imprisonment!

Against all odds, the church has flourished. This is a phenomenon that has become ingrained in the Christianity of China. As pressure from the government has lightened, they do not see themselves returning to former patterns. One Chinese Christian shares his perspective.

> One such community has been meeting since 1969: eight Christian families living in a five-house compound opening up to an inner court. They meet in one of the houses, the covered porch, and the open court. In the winter, they squeeze all the elderly people inside and the young people pack themselves into the porch. Since early 1980 when the government announced that the policy of religious freedom guaranteed by the constitution would be put into practice, they have had three services each Sunday. As a result, many people have been coming to worship.
>
> We are still worshiping in homes . . .The only church building left standing has no roof and it is some six kilometers away. I don't see the possibility of erecting a new church.[12]

---

12. Raymond Fung, *Household of God on China's Soil* (Geneva: World Council of Churches, 1982), N.P. quoted in Thomas Goslin II, *The Church without Walls* (Pasadena, CA: Hope Publishing House, 1984), pp. 49-50.

One of the most significant house church movements has grown to over eighteen thousand house churches in a span of ten years, with over two hundred thousand baptisms.[13] This is not just a house church strategy, it is an aggressive evangelism strategy that is based on sharing the gospel through relational connections of new Christians. It seeks to apply the Great Commission in a very intentional way through a three-part strategy,

1. Go, not come. The focus does not lie on asking people to come to pre-established forms of church meetings. The intent is to go to them and meet them with the gospel. And then take house church meetings to their setting, whether it is in the dorms of a factory, an apartment, or a village hut.
2. Everybody, not just some. All are challenged to share their faith, especially new Christians who are challenged to identify five people with whom they can share their testimony within twenty-four hours after becoming a Christian.
3. Make trainers, not just church members. When Jesus said to "make disciples," he did not mean learners. He meant something more akin to a "trainer." Kai writes, "A disciple must learn everything that his teacher teaches him. Then he needs to follow and to teach others."[14]

In other words, a disciple is not just someone who learns how to get his own life straight before God. He actually learns from his trainer and follows in the footsteps of his trainer to become

---

13. Steve Smith and Ying Kai, *T4T: A Discipleship ReRevolution* (Monument CO: Wigtake Resources, 2011), p. 21.

14. Smith and Kai, p. 49.

a trainer of others. In practical terms, this means that everyone is empowered to be a house church leader wherever they are sharing the gospel.

HOUSE CHURCHES IN INDIA

The work of western missionaries in India has resulted in some of the most significant and widely read missiological thinkers of the day. Lesslie Newbigin was one of them and while most of his mission work focused on more traditional forms of church life, he made an observation that has become a precursor to the development of house church networks throughout India. In 1963, he penned,

> I have lived and worked as a missionary within the structure typical of modern missions, responsible for the conduct of institutions, for the supervision of Indian workers, for the employment and control of teachers and others in charge of congregations. I have seen this system come to a practical standstill: funds were not available to increase the number of salaried workers. . . Only if some fresh resources came from "home" could the mission become a mission again. As it was, it was plain that any talk of "winning India for Christ" was not serious. I was compelled to ask myself whether it is really true that the church's obedience to the Great Commission is intended to be contingent upon the accident of a budgetary surplus.
>
> The answer came through various experiences. Firstly, through seeing how ordinary lads from village congregations . . . could themselves become active witnesses and evangelists among their comrades. Secondly, through learning to call on the services of all kinds of

> lay men and women as volunteer pastors and evangelists for the village congregations left without the guidance of a full-time worker. And thirdly, most decisively, through the experience of a small group-movement in a very backward area where the Gospel had only recently been preached for the first time . . .
>
> The result of this, in the area of which I am speaking, was that the churches began to multiply themselves by a kind of spontaneous growth which was not dependent upon increasing outside resources. In an area almost entirely pagan, the number of Christian congregations rose from thirteen to fifty-five in twelve years . . .In the midst of a movement of this kind, one could speak seriously about winning India for Christ.[15]

What Newbigin observed in embryo form during the middle of the twentieth century has matured into a grand movement throughout parts of the country. Garrison observed,

> A missionary strategist assigned to a North Indian people group found just 28 churches among them in 1989. By the year 2000, a church planting movement had erupted, catapulting the number of churches to more than 4500 with an estimated 300,000 baptized believers."[16]

This is just one of many examples of how house churches are multiplying.

---

15. Lesslie Newbigin, *Trinitarian Doctrine for Today's Mission* (London: Paternoster Press, 1998), pp. 74-75,77.

16. Garrison, p. 17.

Another explosive house church network is led by Victor Choudhrie, a former cancer surgeon. In five years, he has seen the emergence of over one hundred thousand churches.[17] Victor has observed how his churches stand in stark contrast to the traditional church patterns of India. He observes that two of the primary reasons for this are found in the fact that they are seeing a new kind of training and a new kind of Christianity. First, the training is not dependent upon formal Bible schools and sending future leaders off to get an education by the Christian establishment. Instead they are equipped through short training experiences and just-in-time learning. Secondly, this kind of Christianity is different than what they had formerly known. Choudhrie writes,

> In the house churches, "one-man" ministry and "one-day" meetings do not happen. Rather, church life is based on participatory meetings and practical ministry. The activities include apostolic teaching, fellowship (koinonia), table fellowship, prayer, signs and wonders, and sharing of material resources. Shared meals and breaking bread from house-to-house are an integral part of the gatherings. . . .These little house churches in India are like starfish, the more you divide them the more they replicate.[18]

HOUSE CHURCHES IN ETHIOPIA

In the 1950s, Mennonite missionaries helped to establish an indigenous church in Ethiopia. While the church was not modeled on western patterns, it still focused primarily on

---

17. Victor Choudhrie, "Case Study (India): How 100,000 House Churches Were Started in Five Years" in Rad Zdero, *Nexus: The World House Church Movement Reader* (Pasadena, CA: William Carey Library, 2007), p. 304.

18. Ibid., pp. 307-308.

worshipping as a centralized church. And it grew to fourteen congregations of about five thousand believers in 1982. That is when everything changed.

Even though the Marxist-Leninist dictator, Mengistu Haile Mariam, had assumed control in 1974, he waited until 1982 to crack down on this particular church. But when he did, his whip was cruel. Public worship was forbidden, leaders were imprisoned, and officials tracked and stalked parishioners to catch them if they happened to hold religious gatherings. While Muslim and Christian Orthodox congregations were allowed to meet publicly, for some reason the radical nature of this church threatened the government in some way.

Semsu, one of the first church leaders to be imprisoned, recounts,

> We were put in a place in a room with dimensions of less than four by four meters, and I was the last one to come in the cell, and already there [were] 31 individuals in the room. The sleeping situation was tight—head to foot. During the night, if you want to change, you can't turn from right to left, there is no space so you have to ask the cooperation of others. And it was an interesting room where they had no window. Only one door. On top of the door they have a little opening where they have barred space for breathing ventilation. When you have somebody sick with diseases, it was very, very tough. We brought the sick one to that opening space where he could put his nose to breathe. Otherwise, the air was not sufficient for him.[19]

19. "Case Study (Ethiopia): How an Underground Church Survived Persecution" in Rad Zdero, *Nexus*, p. 331.

At this point, the leaders who were not in prison worked to reorganize the church into home groups. They divided church members into groups based on geographic areas. Five people were assigned to groups, and no group ever knew about the meeting times or places of any other group in order to keep the underground system a secret. Only a few leaders were in the know. These leaders kept information from the people so they could honestly say that they did not know about the other functions of the church.[20] Within six weeks after the closing of the church by the government, the central congregation of two thousand people in Addis Ababa was meeting in hundreds of homes in the city. This strategy expanded throughout the fourteen congregations.

In 1992, the communist regime fell and the church was free to reconvene publicly. The church had grown through the house groups from five thousand to fifty thousand. When the doors of the church were closed, there were fourteen congregations, but ten years later there were fifty-three. The communist rule had forced the church to reshape itself and the results were ongoing, even after they were free to return to old patterns. The church continued to emphasize the home groups while at the same time celebrating as a large church with public worship, thereby operating with a cell church structure. In his book that chronicles the story of Meserete Kristos Church, Nathan Hege writes,

> The small group is a way to cope with discipling some twenty thousand new people joining the church each year. Hailu [a young leader in the church] said we should never think of the church as totally free. Satan is always

---

20. Nathan B. Hege, *Beyond Our Prayers* (Scottsdale, PA: Herald Press, 1998), p. 196.

trying to defeat the elect, and constant vigilance and prayer are needed to keep the evil one at bay.[21]

HOUSE CHURCHES IN AMERICA

The conventional church in America is in a state of rapid decline with a weekly net loss of some forty-eight churches.[22] In contrast, house churches have undergone a resurgence and involve some twenty million people, who desire to experiment with a new, yet old, form of Christian church.[23] The reasons are varied: a desire for closer fellowship; a passion for simpler ways of evangelism, discipleship, and church planting; freer forms of spontaneous and participatory worship meetings; and/or a desire to return to basic New Testament patterns.

There are numerous networks dotting the landscape of America, composed of a variety of theologies, demographics, sizes, and styles. Steve Atkerson, Neil Cole, Tony and Felicity Dale, Robert Fitts, Sr., Larry Kreider, Frank Viola, Rad Zdero, and Jon Zens are some of the chief proponents of the North American house church movement, who are both writing about this topic and leading house church movements.[24] Well-known pollster George Barna has estimated that by the year 2025, membership in the conventional church will be cut by fifty percent, while alternative movements (like house churches) will potentially involve thirty to thirty-five percent of all Christians

---

21. Ibid., p. 209.

22. Kreider, p. 67.

23. George Barna, "House Church Involvement Is Growing," June 19, 2006, www.barna.org.

24. Zdero, *Nexus*.

in the nation.[25] Similar movements of house churches are also rising up in other western nations like Australia, Austria, Canada, Finland, Germany, the Netherlands, Spain, Switzerland, and the U.K.[26, 27]

LESSONS LEARNED

- The modern house church movement was partly a reaction to stagnate missionary methods that depended on trained foreigners who were paid a ministerial salary to run the mission organizations and plant churches.
- House church ministry prioritizes the indigenous people of the native country to minister without having to be paid.
- The modern day global house church movement has resulted in spontaneous multiplication of churches and has proven to be one of the most significant influences of the modern-day church.
- China, India, Ethiopia, and America are modern day examples of organic church planting movements that mirror the house church planting movement of the first century.
- House churches can grow in a wide variety of circumstances, such as persecution, poverty, and prosperity.

---

25. George Barna, *Revolution* (Carol Stream, IL: Tyndale House Publishers, 2005), p. 49.

26. Wolfgang Simson, *The House Church Book* (Carol Stream, IL: Tyndale House Publishers, 2009), p. 168.

27. Zdero, pp. 294-381.

Chapter 14

SMALL GROUPS IN NORTH AMERICA

When North Americans hear about the incredible growth of cells and house churches overseas, they often stare back blankly, wondering inwardly why the same isn't happening in North America. Many pastors have even made multiple pilgrimages to David Cho's huge cell church in South Korea, hoping to bring back similar results to North America. The results have been disappointing. Overseas culture and revival is so different.

One person who has tried hard to bridge the small group gap between the East and the West is church growth consultant Carl George. In 1991, he wrote an influential book entitled *Prepare Your Church for the Future.* In this book and the ones that followed, he reimagined principles of the cell phenomenon overseas to North American church and culture. George used creative, modern "North American" language to explain the cell phenomenon so common in "overseas churches." George, however, wasn't the only one attempting to make small groups relevant to North American at the end of the twentieth century.

In fact, in the last thirty years, there's been a proliferation of books on small groups in North America. Many North American Christian authors, seeing the positive potential of small groups for Christian growth and discipleship, have produced a multitude of literature which extols the virtues of small groups in general. Two Christian organizations, Serendipity and Navigators, developed numerous books and study guides on small group ministry. After listing twenty innovations in the modern American church scene, church growth analyst Lyle Schaller wrote,

> Perhaps most important of all, is the decision by tens of millions of teenagers and adults to place a high personal priority on weekly participation in serious, in-depth, lay-led, and continuing Bible study and prayer groups.[1]

While the cell church approach (focus of next chapter) and house church movement (previous chapter) have impacted the North American setting, these movements have had their

1. Lyle E. Schaller, *The New Reformation: Tomorrow Arrived Yesterday* (Nashville, TN: Abingdon Press, 1995), p. 14.

greatest influence overseas.[2] In the western context, three other streams of small group life have had a long-term impact on the western church, and of those three, Carl George's contribution called the *Meta Church model* has been the most influential. Before laying out the history and background to the Meta Church model, there are two others that have served as precursors. The first being the Covenant model.

THE COVENANT MODEL

The main spokesperson of this model—primarily in the 1970s and 1980s—has been Roberta Hestenes.[3] The definition for this model is the following: "A Christian group is an intentional face-to-face gathering of three to twelve people on a regular time schedule with the common purpose of discovering and growing in the possibilities of the abundant life in Christ."[4]

From the definition it is obvious that this type of group is directed toward committed believers. One of the major goals is to create long-term community, and there is a need for strong

---

2. I wrote a book on the cell church movement in North America called *The Church That Multiplies: Growing a Healthy Cell Church in North America* (2005, 2007). In this book, I examine how to make cell church relevant to North American culture without compromising key cell values. I also highlight some thirty-four North American cell churches that are exemplary. However, I'm also keenly aware that cell church ministry is generally harder in western cultures because of individualism, materialism, and traditional church structures. In fact, the motivation to do cell ministry in North America is because of the biblical base, not because of rapid church growth.

3. Roberta Hestenes, *Using the Bible in Groups* (Philadelphia: Westminster Press, 1983).

4. Lyman Coleman, *Serendipity Leadership Conference Syllabus* (Serendipity Publishers, 1993), p. 4:5.

commitment and a high level of accountability. The word *covenant* in this model refers to the commitments or promises that were established in the Old Testament between God and his people. One major focal point is that the group makes a commitment (covenant) to fulfill particular goals, purposes, study topics, ground rules, and logistical details.[5]

Although strong on Christian responsibility and commitment, Coleman makes a wise observation, "Unchurched, non-Christians would not be interested in this type of group. There is no mechanism built into the system for the covenant groups to multiply, or to close with honor. Frequently, covenant groups will last until they die a horrible death."[6]

Covenant groups have a high commitment level, and therefore they are very beneficial for spiritual growth. However, due to the lack of cell multiplication and their closed system, this model is probably the least effective from a church growth standpoint. At the same time, this model has had significant impact upon established churches in North America. In a culture which has been built upon the values and practices of individualism, the Covenant model has proven an effective way of helping disparate people get connected and enter into life together.

THE SERENDIPITY MODEL

The founder of this approach is Lyman Coleman, who has been a small group leader for some four decades. Coleman was especially influenced by Sam Shoemaker, who was the rector of

---

5. Ibid., p. 4:5-4:7

6. Ibid., p. 4:7.

Calvary Episcopal Church in New York City. Bill Wilson, the founder of Alcoholics Anonymous, credits Shoemaker as the primary source for the AA 12-step program. Sam believed that all of the people around his church were his parish. His church grew in its vision to reach out to the entire parish. This vision to reach all people has greatly influenced Lyman Coleman. He says, "The heart of the Serendipity model is the broken people at the door . . . the intention is to create a small group system where people outside the church can find a place of entry and be transformed."[7]

The Serendipity model is best understood by the characteristics that distinguish it from other models:

1. There is a definite beginning and end to each small group. Although his earlier model consisted of a shorter length for each group, later Coleman promoted a one-year group cycle. He says, "The end is marked by a period of releasing where everyone responds to his new calling."[8]
2. There are options that can be chosen in a democratic fashion. People can be in a group whether or not they are members of the church or even attend the worship services. Coleman believes that this is distinct from David Cho's model, explained in the last chapter.
3. The promotion of a wide variety of small groups. He says, "This model can also include traditional Sunday school, where people who are already involved can find a place for sharing and caring."[9] Finally, it is a collegiate

7. Ibid., p. 4:19.

8. Ibid., p. 21.

9. Ibid., p. 21.

> system of small groups. Coleman's approach is similar to the Sunday school system where there was a definite departure from one class and entrance into another class.

The influence of Lyman Coleman on the North American small group scene is significant, with one of his greatest contributions being the *Serendipity Bible for Groups*, which included study questions for every major section of the Scriptures.

THE META-CHURCH MODEL

Carl George was a pastor of an independent Baptist congregation in Gainesville, Florida in the 1970s. While trying to lead his growing church as a whole, he realized that he was asking people to connect with one another when they had very little to nothing in common. Therefore he started a small-group experiment. He identified twelve men whom he thought would make good leaders, and he prayed over the list. Soon thereafter, he cast the vision for leading groups and asked people to pray to see if they could make a commitment to lead such a group. The twelve men on his list all volunteered. This launched George on a journey of small groups that has touched tens of thousands of churches, including some of the largest churches in America.[10]

In 1978, George found that his soul was troubled. After a long contemplation, George's wife, Grace, asked him, "If you were to use the gifts God has given you in ministry, what would you be doing?" To this Carl reacted, "I would be a church analyst. I would be a church consultant." Fourteen hours later, Dr. Peter Wagner called him and asked if he would serve as the director

---

10. Personal interview with Carl George, June 4, 2014.

of the Fuller Institute of Evangelism and Church Growth, a seminar and consulting firm that trained church leaders in the principles of church growth.[11] This gave George the platform to research small-group strategies and test his principles.

George's Meta Church strategy was influenced through his research. The first strategy developed out of his observations made at Yoido Full Gospel Church in Seoul, South Korea. When he visited, he saw the obvious focus on the small group structure, but his analytical skills gave him the ability to see beneath the surface. He observed all of the systems that Cho and his leaders had developed to support the life of the groups. At that time, many American pastors were traveling to Korea and came back with grand ideas about developing groups, but they did not have a vision for developing the systems. This need for systems became central to George's model.

The second major influence on his research was the church growth theory that had been developed by Donald McGavran and Peter Wagner. The four primary questions of church growth shape the way he writes about groups:

1. What are the causes of church growth?
2. What are the barriers to church growth?
3. What are the factors that lead to Christian movements?
4. What principles of church growth are reproducible?[12]

---

11. This story is recounted in Carl F. George and Robert E. Logan, *Leading and Managing Your Church* (Grand Rapids, MI: Revel 1987), pp. 19-20.

12. Gary McIntosh, "Church Movements of the Last Fifty Years in the USA: Four Major Church Movements." Available at: http://churchgrowthnetwork.

With church growth questions like these in mind, George was drawn to study how to make the world-wide cell church paradigm relevant to a North American audience.

A third influence was the first major small-group based church in North America, New Hope Community in Portland, Oregon, which in the 1980s was the best representation of the Korean cell model in a western context. George studied New Hope and worked with Dale Galloway, and even helped them identify some of the needed systems required to support the small groups. Out of this arose seminar resources and his own books on small groups.

NEW HOPE COMMUNITY CHURCH

Dale Galloway started New Hope Community Church in Portland, Oregon in 1972, but it wasn't until 1978 that Galloway visited Seoul, South Korea, to study small groups in Cho's church. He caught a vision for what his church could become through cell ministry and at one time had some five hundred groups. Lyman Coleman refers to Dale Galloway's church as the major advocate of the Cho model in the U.S.[13]

However, it is probably more accurate to describe the New Hope Community Church as the first prototype Meta Church model of small group ministry. His church was based on a wide assortment of small groups. Carl George studied Galloway's church before writing his *Meta Church model.* The small groups at New Hope Community Church were divided into three distinct types:

---

13. Coleman, p. 5:19.

1. Nurture groups
2. Support groups
3. Task groups

The nurture groups provide most of the pastoral care in the church. The support groups were instruments of healing, while the task groups gathered people who were performing diverse types of service. There was even an entire district of groups involved in the church's music ministry. Along with the nurture groups, the task groups met together for sharing, prayer, and Bible application. George Hunter observed, "Every group has an empty chair, as a symbol of the group's mission to reach at least one new person every six months."[14]

The training of small group leaders was very important in this model. Galloway said it well, "The most important job of the pastor and the pastoral staff is leadership development, training lay leaders who will build small groups. Leadership development is essential, and it must be top priority. It cannot be left to chance."[15] Galloway offered a Superbowl event three times a year in which any group member could attend. From these Superbowl events, future leaders emerged who faced the challenge of raising up their own group. Once the new group was formed, the leaders were required to attend a weekly training event where they were given the notes to the pastor's message and discussion questions for Bible application.[16]

---

14. Ibid., pp. 86-87.

15. Dale Galloway, *The Small Group Book* (Grand Rapids: Fleming H. Revell, 1995), p. 118.

16. Coleman, p. 5:19.

GEORGE'S BOOKS

As mentioned earlier, Carl George's first book was entitled *Prepare Your Church for the Future*. The underlying thrust of George's thinking is that because small group ministry has worked so effectively in large churches, it should be adapted to work in any size church, whether in North America or overseas. His overriding emphasis throughout the book is that our current models of church ministry simply do not provide sufficient quality care to sustain a growing church.

His first book comes very close to describing the *cell approach* used in most cell churches around the world. Throughout the book, he describes the home cell group and its contribution to both quality and quantitative growth. The book had a powerful impact on the North American church scene because George gave fresh North American terminology to cell-based concepts.[17]

In his second title, *The Coming Church Revolution*, George redefines the Meta Church model. Instead of promoting a model, he writes about a way to analyze a church,

> Meta-Church thinking examines the degree to which a church has been "cellularized," and its leadership linked. . . . It tries to discern the degree to which group leaders are in fact convening their people, and the degree to which coaches are in fact working with group leaders. The Meta-Church, then . . . is an X ray

17. Carl George, *Prepare Your Church for the Future* (Grand Rapids: Revel, 1991), pp. 57-84.

> to help you look at what you have in order to figure out what's missing.[18]

The Meta Church model then is a way of discerning the degree of small group involvement in a church. George insists throughout *The Coming Church Revolution* that the meta approach is simply a way of seeing what you already have. He spends most of the time describing his mapping strategy called the *meta globe*. This is George's attempt to categorize all groups in the church within certain boundaries. This categorization is supposed to help a church examine their real structure.

Three other distinct differences are made clear in *The Coming Church Revolution*. First, small groups are defined by size rather than components. For example, George says, "Cells include Sunday-School classes, ministry teams, outreach teams, worship-production teams, sports teams, recovery groups, and more . . . any time sixteen or fewer people meet together, you have a small-group meeting."[19] He redefines the Sunday school, as an "on premises" cell system.[20] Second, cell ministry should be introduced unobtrusively in the church. According to George, it is not wise to tell the board when you introduce the cell ministry.[21] Third, in his earlier work he recommended a bimonthly leadership gathering,[22] but in the second book George says that it is possible not to have this meeting, if

---

18. Carl George, *The Coming Church Revolution* (Grand Rapids, Revel, 1994), pp. 279-280.

19. Ibid., pp. 69-70.

20. Ibid., p. 284.

21. Ibid., p. 259.

22. Ibid., pp. 135-145.

the basic structures and principles exist somewhere else in the church.[23]

KEY CHARACTERISTICS OF THE META-CHURCH MODEL

The primary characteristic of this model is found in its diversity of groups. David Tan observes,

> For the Meta-Church any type of groups within the church constitute the cells. All these groups may have different agendas and purposes. The main principle is to involve as many members as possible in groups. Since . . . the agenda of every group cannot be identical, the goal of the Meta-Church is accommodation.[24]

Three common types of groups that most frequently have surfaced in the meta churches are task groups (focus: a particular ministry), fellowship groups (focus: personal care), and discipleship groups (focus: spiritual growth). The emphasis on variety also extends to the life of the groups. Some groups continue indefinitely while other groups may only last a few weeks. Again, it depends on the purpose of the group or the vision of the leader. Within these different types of groups, there are some common threads. They include:

1. Flexibility: Freedom of choice is highly esteemed and emphasized. The top leadership is careful not to assert too much pressure.

---

23. Ibid., p. 203.

24. Tan, p. 18.

2. Leadership Training: All of the churches using the Meta Church model feature some kind of ongoing leadership training, but there is a great degree of flexibility.

Another characteristic relates to the coaching or supervision found in effective small group churches. Each group leader has someone to whom he or she is accountable. That person (called by various names) is assigned to oversee no more than five cell leaders. Over the leader of five is another leader to whom the leader of five is accountable, and the process continues.

One way to better understand the Meta Church model is to contrast it with the cell church strategy (next chapter), as the following table attempts to do:

	Meta Church	**Cell Church**
Types of groups	Any type of group is acceptable in the Meta Church model. Small groups are loosely defined	The cell group is similar in vision, focus, format, and purpose. The cell definition is very important
Small Groups/ Church Program and Ministries	There is no conflict between the small groups and ministries because oftentimes the small groups are part of the church supported programs or ministries	The cell groups are the base of the church and all are expected to participate. People are first encouraged to be in a holistic cell group. From there, some will also participate in church ministries
Lead Pastor and Team	Could possibly delegate this ministry to an associate pastor and still maintain the small group program	Must be guiding the cell vision in order to guarantee succes
Coaching / Supervision	Loose and flexible with some light control	Organized, directed to ensure quality control
Leadership Training	Some kind of ongoing training, although flexible and loosely organized	Closely monitored with ongoing training

The Meta Church influence has impacted and continues to influence how churches function. Carl George has either directly or indirectly taught numerous large churches in America, including two of the most influential, Willow Creek Community Church in South Barrington, Illinois and Saddleback Community Church in Lake Forest, California. There is much that we can learn from the journey of the Meta Church, but there is more to the story, which we'll learn about in the next chapter.

LESSONS LEARNED

- Three key small group models in the U.S. are the Covenant model, Serendipity model, and Meta Church model. All three have adapted small group principles to fit within North American culture. All three small group models highlight diversity and flexibility.
- The Covenant model is more focused on discipleship, whereas the Serendipity model is very creative, emphasizing start and stop times.
- The Meta Church model, established by Carl George, is the most widely used U.S. model, and is characterized by variety and accommodation. Small groups include Sunday school classes, ministry teams, outreach groups, worship-production teams, sports groups, recovery groups, and house groups—groups being defined as any meeting of sixteen or fewer people.
- Leadership development is a primary goal of Meta Church model thinking.

Chapter 15

THE CELL CHURCH MOVEMENT

On a Sunday evening in the summer of 1964, Yonggi Cho, a young Korean pastor, collapsed on the platform of his church. The then twenty-seven years old Cho had reached a point of utter physical exhaustion.

Earlier in the day he had preached at the morning services and then baptized three hundred new converts. After picking up an American evangelist from the airport, he was interpreting for him in the evening service when his breakdown occurred. His church had grown from four to two thousand four hundred members. Although assisted by his mother-in-law, Jashil

Choi, and missionary John Hurston, Cho had shouldered an almost impossible ministry burden at the growing church. He had preached at the two Sunday morning services, mid-week services, and attended daily early morning prayer meetings. He also took it upon himself to counsel and perform all weddings and funerals. Crumpled on the stage that summer evening, he whispered to Hurston, "John, I'm dying."[1]

Cho felt God had called him to grow the largest church in the world, yet he attempted to do this in his own strength. After being rushed to the hospital and examined, the doctor told Cho's associates,

> This man is physically exhausted. His health has been broken, and his heart is weak. To recover, he will require total bed rest. After that it would be my suggestion that he find another line of work. It would be better if he never preached or pastored again. The strain could kill him.[2]

In spite of his depleted strength, Cho attempted to continue as usual. Against the wishes of others, he tried to preach in the first service of his church the following Sunday but fainted after just eight minutes. In the second service he again tried to preach but lasted only five minutes before again collapsing. In the weeks and months that followed, Cho cried out to God from his sick bed for healing, but God didn't seem to answer. In his book *Successful Home Cell Groups,* Cho recounts that he was blindly claiming the promises of healing in the Bible

---

1. David Yonggi Cho, with Harold Hostetler, *Successful Home Cell Groups* (South Plainfield, NJ: Bridge Publishing, 1981), p. 11.

2. Karen Hurston, *Growing the World's Largest Church* (Springfield, MO: Gospel Publishing House, 1994), p. 83.

without ever seeking God's will. On one occasion, however, he prayed, "Father, you gave all of these promises to us. But I claim them and you don't heal me. Aren't you going to heal me?" Immediately Cho was startled by an inaudible but clear voice. "Son, I am going to heal you, but the healing is going to take ten years."[3]

Little did Cho realize at that time that the desperate situation he found himself in would not only change his church but set in motion a revolution in ecclesiology that would transform churches around the world. God wanted the rest of the church world to know that a single pastor can't really care for a church, let alone a church of over two thousand people.[4] Through Cho, God was about to birth the modern day cell movement.

Cho felt a strong call to pastor, and he had a vision to grow a colossal church that would be the biggest in all of Korea. Yet his devastated health dictated that he could not carry out his pastoral responsibilities in the only way he knew how. As Cho lay in his bed, he searched the Scriptures to see how the early church ministered to thousands of new believers. Cho was struck by how these early Christians met from house-to-house in small groups to worship and fellowship. Likewise, he noticed how Moses in Exodus 18:13-26 divided the millions into divisions and small groups of ten people.

---

3. Cho, p. 11.

4. Cho's situation is a lot like the story of Gideon (Judges 6). God wanted to glorify himself through Gideon, so he asked Gideon to reduce his men. If Gideon maintained a large army, he could have boasted in his great strength, power, and military might. God wanted to make sure that Gideon only boasted in God's greatness, so he whittled his strength down to the bare minimum. God reduced Cho to nothing, so God would get all the glory.

Cho didn't originally catch the cell vision for church growth's sake. It wasn't a clever way to grow a church larger and larger. Rather, he realized that he was growing his church in an unbiblical, human-centered way that eventually caused him to wind up in the hospital. Following these biblical insights, Cho devised a plan to divide his congregation into home groups under the leadership of his deacons, who were the male lay ministers. They rejected the idea, however, and Cho ended up taking his plan to the women lay leaders who agreed to do it. In Korea at that time, males dominated leadership positions both in the church and culture. So for Cho to launch his cell vision through women was equally radical and gave God increased glory.[5]

Under Cho's close supervision and instruction, twenty home cell groups were initially launched by these women. The groups encountered various difficulties at first, and it would have been easy for Cho to drop his new plan. However, he felt God had told him that he wouldn't be healed for ten years, and he had no other plan except the one God had given him.[6]

---

5. It's also true that Cho's cell transition was started and motivated by female cell leaders. This was great in the beginning and was a very important phenomenon. However, Cho didn't do much to become a male oriented cell church, and it seems that the male attendance in cells fell far behind the female attendance. When I visited in 1997, there were nineteen thousand female led cell groups and about six thousand male led groups. When I was at Yoido, I noticed that the males enjoyed the Sunday morning programs and offices where they could sit and associate with other males.

6. Those who make it in cell ministry have a deep conviction of the rightness of the strategy. They've heard from God, believe cell ministry is firmly based in Scripture, and are ready to overcome all the struggles and difficulites that arise. Those who don't make it cell ministry are often just "testing the water" to see if their church will grow faster.

In the months and years that followed, Cho refined his growing cell system. Initially, his church and its new methodology was easily overlooked, but in 1974 the church moved to a larger facility on Yoido Island and assumed the name Yoido Full Gospel Church. At that time there were 16,000 members in 542 cell groups. In its first year in the new location, they added 3000 members. In 1976 the mushrooming church reported 1600 cells.[7]

While a version of this story opens the introduction of this book, Cho's testimony is worth repeating because of its impact on the worldwide cell church movement. In fact, one common pattern in the largest worldwide cell churches is the influence of David Cho. All have mentioned their indebtedness to Cho, and all but one of them was initially inspired to do cell ministry because of Cho's teaching and example.[8] The pastors of the two largest cell churches, as well as the most influential pastors in Latin America, visited Cho's church before starting their own cell ministry.[9] The inspiration of Cho is also seen in the writings of the top cell experts today.[10] Hadaway observes,

---

7. Hurston, p. 191.

8. For more on this topic, see Joel Comiskey's Ph.D. dissertation http://www.joelcomiskeygroup.com/articles/dissertation/index.html. The exception was Love Alive Church in Tegucigalpa, Honduras. This church started using small groups in 1974 and only later heard about Cho's church.

9. I am referring to César Castellanos, founding pastor of La Misión Carismática Internacional, in Bogota, Colombia, and Sergio Solórzano, founding pastor of La Misión Cristiana Elim, in San Salvador, El Salvador.

10. Ralph Neighbour, Carl George, and Dale Galloway all liberally quote Cho as the foundation for their particular model of cell ministry. In George's *Prepare Your Church for the Future*, Cho or Cho's church appears on thirteen pages. In George's, *The Coming Church Revolution*, Cho is mentioned on nine pages. A similar pattern appears in Neighbour's book, *Where Do We Go from Here,* and Galloway's book, *20/20 Vision.*

> The word spread that Paul Cho's church and several other huge churches in Seoul reached their massive size through home cell groups and that the technique will work anywhere. A movement began, and pastors have flocked to Korea to learn. . . . Churches all over the world are beginning to adopt the home cell group as an organizational tool. . . .[11]

Although many churches encouraged by Cho adopted the cell methodology and succeeded, many more attempted cell groups and failed, or had few visible results. Many churches started cells for the wrong motivation. They simply wanted to grow their church like Cho and didn't understand how to apply cell principles to their own context. They also failed to take into account the revival atmoshpere of Korea and many other characteristics that helped Cho's church become so large.

Cho himself has pondered why cell ministry does or doesn't work in other places. The reasons he has given in his books and articles include:

1. Failure of the senior pastor to provide leadership of the cell system.
2. Failure to learn the cell method thoroughly.
3. Inadequate training and support of group leaders. Cho believes that supervision of cell leaders is critical.
4. Lack of evangelistic focus in the cell groups.
5. Failure of the pastor to relinquish authority and ministry.

---

11. Hadaway, Wright, and DuBose, p. 17.

Not only has Cho's church successfully implemented cell ministry, there are approximately nine additional churches in Korea that have reached a membership of thirty thousand or more. All of them, without exception, have structured their churches around cell group ministry. There is no doubt that Cho's church has had a significicnat influence around the world and continues to do so today.

CHURCH GROWTH INTERNATIONAL

One significant visitor to Yoido Full Gospel Church was Dr. Donald McGavran, the founder of the church growth movement. Cho's cell church explosion came in the midst of the church growth era at Fuller Theological Seminary. It was an age when pastors excitedly looked and studied the growing cell churches around the world and were not hesitant to test the model in their own churches. McGavran encouraged Cho to hold seminars to instruct the many pastors that were visiting the church.

In 1976, Church Growth International (CGI) was born under the leadership of John Hurston. Tens of thousands of pastors from every part of the world have attended the annual conferences of CGI. Cho's book *Successful Home Cell Groups,* published in 1982, has also been pivotal in the diffusion of the movement.[12] Peter Wagner, successor to Donald McGavran

---

12. I first heard Cho speak in 1984 at a church growth conference at Fuller Seminary, and from that time forth I developed a passion for cell ministry. I sat in amazement as Cho reeled off story after story of the amazing church growth in Korea and how Yoido Full Gospel Church could pastor all of the five hundred thousand members through the eighteen thousand cell groups. I bought all of Cho's tapes, listened to them over and over, and tried to implement cell ministry in my own church plant.

at Fuller Seminary, became part of the board at CGI and has faithfully attended the conferences since they started.

It's interesting that God would choose the oppressed nation of South Korea to give birth to the modern cell church movement. The history of Korea is one of the world's most turbulent sagas of a small nation's struggle for survival against seemingly impossible odds. From the seventh century onwards, Korea has come under the control of both China and Japan. In 1945, the Japanese surrendered control of Korea to the Americans in the south and to Russia in the north. An uneasy pact was signed which could not prevent subsequent war between North Korea (backed by Russia and China) and South Korea (backed by America). God once again has shown himself strong among those who are weak. This is certainly the case with his choice of Korea to start the cell church phenomenon.

FED UP WITH CHURCHIANITY

Although Cho inspired many of the largest cell churches in the world, the individual who has pioneered cell-based ministry in the U.S. is Ralph Neighbour.[13] In 2014, he turned eighty-five while continuing his cell church leadership in the U.S. and around the world. His zeal and cell passion are captured in the following quote,

> . . . the cell is the church, and the church is the cell. It is the basic building block of the larger community called

---

13. While Neighbour opened up the door for cell ministry in the U.S., he is also very influential worldwide. Neighbour not only popularized cell ministry, he also explained it. This was not true with David Cho. In Latin America, the cell pastors with whom I talked were inspired by Cho, but they lacked concrete instruction from Cho concerning how to run a cell ministry.

> "local church." There must be no competition with it—none at all. Everything in the city-wide structure must exist for the cells, be operated by the cells, and must strengthen the life of the cells. As in the human body, the life of the church is in the cells. Are people to be reached for Christ? It is done through cells. Are people to be built up in Him? It is to be done through cells.[14]

As Cho was just beginning to refine and grow his cell methodology in 1965, Ralph Neighbour was looking for a biblical church structure, rather than the programmed based churches that dotted the landscape. He wrote, "When I turned thirty-six I was absolutely, completely disgusted with traditional church structures that catered to self-needs and ignored the unchurched."[15] Neighbour had already worked with churches in a wide diversity of settings. He grew up as a pastor's child, had worked for the Billy Graham organization in its infancy, planted twenty-three churches in southern Pennsylvania, and had acted as an evangelism consultant for five years for the Texas Baptist Convention.

During these years, Neighbour had become increasingly disillusioned with churches structured for maintenance rather than mission. At forty years old, Neighbour left the comfort of his denominational job to spear-head "an experimental church" in rapidly growing west Houston. He writes,

> In 1969, a non-traditional church in Houston was formed with 38 courageous pioneers. We called ourselves "The People Who Care," and became a "Parable Church." Without knowing what we were doing, we

---

14. Ralph Neighbour, *Where Do We Go from Here* (Houston, TX: Touch Publications, 1990), pp. 68-69.

15. Neighbour Jr., p. 78.

> stumbled into patterns which were being used by other cell group churches we didn't know existed.[16]

Neighbour stumbled onto this model as a pioneer and eventually became its chief spokesman. One significant person impacted by Neighbour was a young Baptist seminary student named Lawrence Khong from Singapore who became involved in the Houston church. He returned to Singapore in the mid-'80s to pastor a growing church and was unexpectedly baptized in the Holy Spirit and spoke in tongues. Baffled by this encounter, which he experienced in the privacy of his own time with the Lord, he shared it with his deacons. Little did he realize that this revelation to his leadership would spell the end of his ministry in a church with traditional Baptist doctrine. He then launched a new church called Faith Community Baptist Church (FCBC) in 1988.

Khong asked Neighbour to guide him and his church into an integrated cell methodology. At first Neighbour did this by dividing his time between Texas and Singapore, but in 1990 he moved to Singapore to become the associate pastor at FCBC. The combination of an outstanding senior pastor—tremendously gifted in speaking and leadership—and the cell strategy spear-headed by Neighbour enabled the church to grow from six hundred to five thousand in attendance with five hundred cell groups between 1988 and Neighbour's return to Houston in 1997. FCBC was an ideal platform for Neighbour because it allowed him to refine his cell strategy and material. FCBC became an exemplary cell church with a model cell church strategy.[17]

---

16. Neighbour, Jr., p. 87.

17. Faith Community Baptist Church also inherited some weaknesses and eventually left the more principle based cell strategy in favor of one particular model.

Neighbour and Khong aggressively shared the cell strategy through the annual international conferences on the cell church which first drew hundreds and then thousands of pastors, missionaries, and leaders from all over the world.[18] Neighbour's cell church manifesto, *Where Do We Go from Here? A Guidebook for the Cell Group Church*, published in 1990, fanned the flames of the cell movement in many countries, including the United States, Canada, Australia, and South Africa. This book greatly accelerated the cell movement in t countries and beyond.

Where Do We Go from Here had a powerful impact because it combined the biblical base for cell ministry, a principle-based analysis of cell churches, and examples of many growing worldwide cell churches. Granted, it was a very idealistic book, and was thought to provide little hope for churches to make the transition to cell ministry in North America. Yet, it stirred the imaginations of those who longed for change and started a movement in North America.

In 1991, Neighbour launched *CellChurch* magazine from his publishing ministry in Houston. This magazine became a unifying voice of the movement. TOUCH Outreach Ministries, the publishing and seminar ministry founded by Neighbour and based in Houston, Texas, and Lawrence Khong's Touch Ministries International in Singapore were international heralds for the cell movement. The prolific, visionary Neighbour through his practical books and magazine gave wind to the movement at a time when an increasing number of pastors and church leaders were becoming disillusioned with the traditional church structure.

---

18. It's often a good idea to see cell ministry in a model cell church and then to read about how to do it. Theory mixed with practice is the best way to demonstrate the effectiveness of cell ministry to make disciples who make disciples.

In 1994, the political foundations of the country of South Africa were crumbling as apartheid was being dismantled and a new multi-racial government was being formed. In the midst of this upheaval there was a new spiritual openness in the country. As political structures were being radically altered, pastors and churches were also looking for new ecclesiastical patterns. At the invitation of Pastor Martin Hopkins of Newcastle, Natal, Dr. Neighbour led three introductory cell church conferences in May 1994 in Pretoria, Newcastle, and Mossel Bay.

These conferences created strong interest in the cell model and in mid-1994 about one hundred and twenty South African pastors came to Singapore to learn from Neighbour at Faith Community Baptist Church. In response to this specially planned training seminar, Neighbour was invited to come to South Africa to give in-depth teaching in cell church methodology. He developed a four-week course with one week being taught each quarter. This training entitled "The Year of Transition" was launched in October 1994 in South Africa and over the next two years would be taught to thousands of pastors. Churches implementing cell groups in South Africa shared their learning and helped further disseminate cell methodology to churches in the nearby countries of Lesotho, Botswana, Malawi, Zimbabwe, as well as countries far away, including Ukraine and the United States.

The Year of Transition (TYOT) training and its successor entitled Advanced Cell Training (ACT) were taught by TOUCH and its affiliated international ministries in many countries, including the United States, Russia, Brazil, the Philippines, El Salvador, Canada, and Australia. TYOT was launched in 1999 and 2000 in England and Germany. Regent University of Virginia Beach, Virginia, in 1996 became the first seminary offering Master's and Doctor of Ministry level degrees with a major in cell ministry. The core of their cell ministry courses were the TYOT and ACT cell curriculum developed by TOUCH.

INFLUENTIAL CELL VOICES

In 1974, Amor Viviente, a charismatic church in Honduras, started by Mennonite missionaries, Ed and Gloria King, began using a home cell system when their meeting place was taken away. When they realized the superiority of the cell structure for evangelism and discipleship, they retained it. This church, which grew to some seven thousands in the year 2000, planted churches throughout its native Honduras and in several U.S. cities. Rene Peñalba, one of the founding pastors, left Amor Viviente to start his own church, which has also grown into a cell-based movement. Many other churches in Honduras have also grown and blossomed. In fact, cell-based ministry has become the new norm through the carefully modeling of cell-based ministry.

Another early pioneer of cell ministry, Wener Kniesel, pastor of Christian Center Buchegg in Zurich, Switzerland began doing cell ministry about the same time Cho started his ministry in the early 1970s. He simultaneously felt that doing cell ministry was the biblical way to do church, so he continued to transition his church in the face of many obstacles. Kniesel said that every step of the transition process was painful for his Zurich, Switzerland congregation, but they eventually became a thriving cell church in the busy secular society of Zurich, Switzerland. The church grew to some three hundred cell groups and has trained pastors and leaders around the world.

In the United States in south central Pennsylvania, Dove Christian Fellowship was birthed in October of 1980 under the leadership of Larry Kreider using a cell methodology. Dove has planted churches in the U.S., New Zealand, France, Scotland, Uganda, Kenya, and Barbados. In 2013, Dove had about one hundred twenty congregations. Dove was an early pioneer that has consistently demonstrated a balanced, biblical basis for their cell ministry. They have since added house church networks to their repertoire of ministry.

Bethany World Prayer Center also adopted the cell strategy in 1996 and became one of the flagship cell churches in North America. Bethany hosted cell conferences each year and many pastors were trained. At one point, Bethany attracted thousands of pastors to its yearly cell conferences promoting "Winning souls and making disciples." Stockstill's book *The Cell Church* came out in 1996 and had an important impact on the cell movement.

CELL-BASED MINISTRY SPREADS IN AFRICA AND ASIA

While Cho was developing his cell system, other churches around the world were catching similar visions and learning from each other.

EPBOM, WEST AFRICA

In 1975, Pastor Dion Robert began using a cell group strategy to start EPBOM (Eglise Protestante Baptiste Oeuvres et Mission Internationale).[19] Ivory Coast is home to eighteen million

---

19. Church is located in Ivory Coast, West Africa; Size: 200,000; Senior Pastor: Dion Robert; Background: Started in 1975, non-denominational EPBOM has fifty-six locations in Abidjan and many more throughout the country in addition to 18,0000 cell groups; Web site: dion.kingdomconnector.com

residents, many of whom are French-speaking and work in agriculture. It's estimated that some thirty-five to forty percent are Muslim; twenty to thirty percent are Christians; and another forty percent practice indigenous beliefs.

After hearing Brother Andrew, who ministered to persecuted Christians in communist countries, Dion desired a church structure that would not be dependent on large meetings, nor centered on the pastor. His initial inspiration for the cell methodology came from the organizational structure that Moses used in Exodus chapter eighteen.[20] Beginning with just three people, his movement grew to 3,180 cells in 1993 in the city of Abidjan and some 1,896 cells in daughter churches in the Ivory Coast, Guinea, Burkina Faso, Benin, and several other African countries and the United States.[21] In 2010 this family of churches claimed a total membership of 200,000.

Pastor Dion Robert asks each member to faithfully attend a cell group and go through the discipleship equipping process, which focuses on transformed lives. African culture has been so thoroughly dominated by animism (the belief in the appeasement of spirits who control all life events) that people for centuries have lived in fear, guilt, and uncertainty. EPBOM has discovered that unless salvation includes breaking the Satanic lies and strongholds caused by animism, believers quickly revert back to past bondage.

---

20. Jim Lassiter, personal email to Jim Egli entitled "Re: Questions." This was a private e-mail message to Jim Egli from Jim Lassiter on June 16, 1999.

21. Dion Yaye Robert, *Cell Group Ministry: One of the Secrets of Church Growth* (Tulsa, Oklahoma: Christian Works and Mission International, 1997), p. 33.

Those at EPBOM know they'll never produce an effective harvest worker who is bound by satanic strongholds. Pastor Dion says,

> In the lives of the sheep there will often be strongholds that need to be torn down. These at times may be demonic hereditary ties or some form of demonization by evil spirits. *Soul therapy* is the process of tearing down ungodly strongholds that include immoral activity, curses, animistic fears and ancestor worship.[22]

This church is well-known for turning enslaved people into flaming evangelists for Jesus Christ that start new home churches.

ABBALOVE CHURCH, JAKARTA, INDONESIA

Abbalove Church started in 1979 when a group of Jakarta college students yearned for a move of God's Spirit. God stirred them to start a church and Eddy Leo, an early team leader, eventually became one of the elders and the lead apostolic ministry member of the movement. The church originally started as a community-based church and then later developed into a cell-based church after the leadership team visited Cho's church in Korea and Faith Community Baptist Church in Singapore.

From the beginning they envisioned the need to develop young people to serve as leaders and change the nation and the world. In 2014, the church had grown to 20,000 people in

---

22. Leslie Brickman, *Preparing the 21st Century Church* (Fairfax, VA: Xulon Press, 2002), pp. 231-247.

the Sunday celebrations and 25,000 in their 2,000 weekly cell groups. Abbalove has become eleven local churches, each with their own elders. Abbalove Church is growing rapidly as they concentrate on unreached peoples and cities. The context of their church is the Indonesian Muslim majority and their desire has been to bless the unreached people with God's love.

Abbalove realizes that the cell is critical to making disciples who make disciples. Everyone is expected to participate in a cell group. The three pillars of the church are: cell, celebration, and personal discipleship. The three pillars can only be established if everyone is equipped continually. Abbalove Church sees itself as helping people on their journey—not as having reached their final destination. By God's grace, the church has never had a division because they have always focused on experiencing Jesus and making sure Jesus is the focus, not ministry.

FAMILY OF GOD CHURCH, SOLO, INDONESIA

Obaja Setiawan went to junior high school in Indonesia in the 1980s. At the time, he had no hair. No one—including the doctors—knew why he lost his hair, and his family couldn't find any legitimate help. He was so embarrassed, he left school. Friends and family urged him to visit witch doctors and try magic potions, but nothing worked. Someone suggested Jesus. "Why not?" He thought. He prayed to Jesus and his hair began growing back. When asked about the new growth, he answered, "It must be the medicine." The hair disappeared, and Obaja quickly realized he had denied Jesus and begged again for mercy. God answered and today Obaja has a full head of black hair.

This miracle impacted Obaja so completely that he promised God that he would serve him all the days of his life. And he did serve God as a successful businessman, actively ministering in his church as a layman and supporting it financially. But in September 1989, God called Obaja to start his own church. He felt so inadequate because his business training didn't include seminary education. Yet, he obeyed and started a cell group that multiplied to include some 20,000 people in 2010.[23]

Pastor Obaja has carried his simple faith message of God's power in weakness. Throughout his ministry he has believed God to work the impossible in weak, human vessels, even in an area where eighty-eight percent of the two hundred fifty million people are Muslim.

In 1999, he traveled to Bogota, Colombia with Eddy Leo to learn about the G-12 strategy at a cell-based church called the International Charismatic Mission. Obaja couldn't speak English or Spanish, and since the conference wasn't translated into his mother tongue, he didn't understand most of what was said in the week-long Bogota conference. He did catch one phrase, however: "Anyone can be a fruitful cell leader." He saw clearly how God wanted him to develop his entire congregation to be ministers rather than hearers.

His dream came true. He often testifies of illiterate people leading others to Christ through cell ministry, discipling them, and then preparing them to lead their own cell groups. Obaja has seen countless poor, uneducated, and desperate rickshaw

---

23. The Family of God Church (GBI); Location: Solo, Indonesia; Size: twenty thousand; Senior Pastor: Obaja Tanto Setiawan; Background: Affiliated with the Church of God, GBI was started in 1989. Now, in addition to its one main location, the church has fifty church plants and one thousand five hundred cell groups; Web site: www.gbika.org

drivers becoming zealous evangelists for Christ who lead new cell groups. The church likes to ask the weakest and the poorest cell leaders to give testimonies of what God has done in their cells through conversion and multiplication. In this way, GBI encourages everyone to step up to the plate, get involved in a cell group, and eventually lead their own. And GBI has a great training process to help potential cell leaders succeed. Their discipleship equipping includes a spiritual retreat, a seminar, and three Bible courses that each person must take in preparation to leading their own cell group. And what's amazing is the location of this church—a Muslim dominated area of Java, Indonesia.

GBI has stimulated many churches to look beyond those who appeared to be the "leader-type" and to see God's power in the weak and lowly. GBI has demonstrated how God does the extraordinary through ordinary, weak people.

GRACE FELLOWSHIP AND CCMN, HONG KONG

Ben Wong started Grace Church in 1987. Wong always had a heart for discipleship, but in 1989, he read Cho's *Successful Home Cell Groups* and realized that the New Testament way to make disciples took place in cell groups. That same year, thirty people from the church visited Ralph Neighbour in Singapore, and they all read Neighbour's book, *The Shepherd's Guidebook*. Neighbour helped tweak Wong's vision and the church began to grow through cell ministry, reaching and growing to some 2,000 by 2006.

Wong wasn't satisfied in just growing his own church larger and larger. He caught the vision to share the cell vision with other pastors in the city, and they began to hold joint conferences, sharing speakers and information. Wong, along with a New Zealand missionary, Neville Chamberlin, felt compelled to connect cell groups with worldwide missions, much like the Moravians had done 275 years earlier. Cell Church Missions Network was born as a way to share resources with other like-minded cell churches and promote worldwide missions.

The Cell Church Missions Network is primarily concerned with mobilizing cell church people to finish the Great Commission. They believe that those who have led and multiplied a cell group are the best missionaries to penetrate the unreached cultures because they've already experienced fruitful ministry in their own culture. The theme of CCMN is "No glory and no control." CCMN has sent out some 175 missionaries between 1997 and 2014 and held over 100 conferences. CCMN missionaries are on thirteen fields, including, Macau, China, Japan, Thailand, Bangladesh, India, Cambodia, Indonesia, Philippines, Pakistan, Turkey, North Africa, and Middle East.[24]

WINDS OF CHANGE FROM SOUTH AMERICA

Two Latin American cell churches derived principles from Yoido Full Gospel Church and then adapted these principles to the cell church strategy that was more effective in their own context. They established a path for many to follow.

ELIM CHURCH, EL SALVADOR

The Elim Church sits in the city of San Salvador. Of the country's nearly seven million Salvadorans, eighty-three percent are

---

24. "100 conferences" refers to some thirteen CCMN summits, approximately thirty missionary and international conferences, and some sixty including regional, national, and coaching conferences.

Catholic; however, an estimated one million are Protestant evangelicals, and this number is growing with the help of a simple, but efficient church called the Elim Church.[25]

Elim is not a fairy tale success story. They've experienced their share of hard knocks and problems. The church weathered a civil war that killed 75,000 and a massive earthquake that devastated the country, killing 100 Elim members. Perhaps the greatest tragedy was the removal of the founding pastor due to a moral failure. Yet, in spite of these odds, the Elim Church has multiplied cell groups throughout El Salvador and around the world.

Elim's growth can be attributed to their passion for Jesus, their persistence in cell group church basics, and their evangelistic penetration that multiplies cells all over the city. Elim's main goal is to penetrate the city through multiplying cell groups. In 2013, some 118,000 people attended the church's eleven thousand cell groups. Those same cell groups rented city buses to travel together to the weekly celebration services to hear God's Word.

Elim defines a cell as a group of three to fifteen adults who meet weekly outside the church building for the purpose of evangelism, community, and spiritual growth with the goal of

---

25. Size: 118,000 in the mother church; (11,000 cells); Senior Pastor: Mario Vega; Background: Started in 1977, Elim is part of a non-denominational movement called Elim International. The church now has 160 churches worldwide, and its annual rally in San Salvador draws some 2,000 people; Web site: elim.org.sv. I first visited the church in 1996 and instantly saw how God has created a new culture at Elim, quite unlike the Latin communities around it. Elim is extremely organized, seeing God's wonderful order in Scripture and believing that God wants them to accurately measure what's happening in their midst.

multiplication. The majority of Elim's cells are family oriented (a mixture of men, women, singles,and so forth), but they also have women's cells, youth cells, and children's cells. The cells are organized geographically, so that each group multiplies within its own geographical area.

Elim's cells first started in 1986, but it was a long process of failure, regrouping, and perfecting their cell system. They kept on pressing on to improve their cell ministry until it worked. God has used Elim to develop a church without walls that penetrates into every corner of the community and raises up harvest workers to continue the process.[26]

TRIP TO KOREA

Sergio Solórzano, born in Guatemala, came to El Salvador to start an Elim Christian Mission Church, a grass roots Evangelical denomination which started in Guatemala.[27] Solórzano started the church in 1977 in a rented house with nine persons. The church grew rapidly and by 1981 there were three thousand people attending the mother church. By 1985, the church had planted some seventy daughter churches around the country, but the attendance at the mother church had stagnated.

---

26. To learn more about the Elim church, read Joel Comiskey's *Passion and Persistence: How the Elim Church's Cell Groups Penetrated an Entire City for Jesus* (Houston, TX: Touch Publications, 2004).

27. The Elim El Salvador no longer recognizes the mother church in Guatemala. Elim El Salvador claims that the mother church in Guatemala no longer believes in the Trinity and teaches other errant doctrines. Interestingly enough, Elim El Salvador now sends missionaries to Guatemala to plant a new brand of Elim churches. It should also be noted that Sergio Solórzano is no longer lead pastor at Elim due to moral failure. Mario Vega is the new lead pastor.

Due to this stagnation, in 1985, Pastor Solórzano visited David Yonggi Cho's church in Korea. He came back convinced that cell group ministry would revolutionize Elim. He called together the pastors of the twenty-five daughter churches around San Salvador and asked them to close down their churches and join with him to form one huge cell church in San Salvador. By 1991, six years later, the cell group attendance had grown to 57,000 with a large proportion attending the Sunday celebration services.[28] In 1996, Sergio Solórzano was asked to step down from the mother church due to his moral failure, and the leadership team asked Mario Vega to lead Elim San Salvador. Mario Vega was with Elim in 1977 when the church first started. He left the mother church in San Salvador on April 14, 1980 to help a small struggling Elim Church in Santa Ana, a province of El Salvador. Under his leadership, Elim Santa Ana grew to some 10,000 people (average cell attendance).

Since Mario took over leadership of Elim San Salvador in 1997, the church continued to grow to 118,000 in 11,000 cell groups. Pastor Mario is excited about what God is doing through Elim and boldly promotes what has worked for them. He realizes, however, that copying a model verbatim rarely works. The Elim Church, in fact, never copied Cho's original cell model exactly. Rather, they have adapted the Korean cell group church model to fit El Salvador's unique circumstances.

UNIQUE FEATURES OF ELIM

Throughout Latin America EC is known for multiplying strong cell groups. Some of the reasons for their cell group strength are:

28. The present facility is located less than one kilometer from the original 1977 meeting place, which is about ten miles from downtown San Salvador.

Team ministry. Each cell has a team that consists of the leader, assistant, host, treasurer, secretary, and members at large. The cell leader's primary goal is to form this core team. The Elim Church is convinced that the success of the cell group depends on the nucleus.

Each cell team meets weekly to plan, pray, dream, and act. After a time of edification, team members plan for the normal Saturday night cell meeting. They decide who will visit straying members, reach new people, and pray for those in need.
Having two separate meetings (one for planning and one for the regular cell) is the major distinction between the cell system at Elim and those at other cell churches.

Statistical tracking. The Elim Church is extremely organized, seeing God's wonderful order in Scripture. They believe God wants them to accurately measure what's happening in their midst. All eighty staff pastors at Elim, for example, can tell you on Tuesday morning what the previous week's numbers are: attendance, conversions, baptisms, people visited, and those trained. And all of these numbers are exact.

Exact statistics are important at Elim because they measure progress toward the goal of penetrating their city for Jesus. It helps each leader to know where they stand, and what they need to improve to more effectively reach the entire city for Jesus.[29] The statistical follow-up of every meeting gives pastors and supervisors a progress report of each cell, and it motivates the leaders to reach out. In addition, the smooth functioning Jethro system provides help and training for cell leaders.

---

29. Elim had virtually no outside missionary influence. Nor was Pastor Sergio Solórzano trained in the United States or Europe.

Friendship evangelism. The most effective form of cell outreach at Elim is friendship evangelism. Leaders instruct their groups to make friends, win their confidence, and then invite them to the meeting. The goal is for those who are befriended to receive Christ and become a disciple through cell ministry.

Josefina López is a good example of this friendship evangelism. She was a Jehovah's Witness for seven years before converting to Christianity through the love and friendship of cell members who just happened to be meeting next door to Josefina's house (approximately 80,000 JWs in El Salvador). Her neighbors befriended her and lovingly invited her to their group, but Josefina refused, remaining true to her cult's calling.

The cell multiplied and formed another one down the street. Then it multiplied again—this time meting behind her house. The neighbors of all three cells tried to love and serve Josefina, inviting her to their groups, but she managed to resist them. She noticed, however, the joy, the vibrant singing, and especially their changed lives. Finally, Josefina decided to attend the cell behind her house, using the excuse of wanting to taste the dessert. God used the leader to clearly present the gospel message, and the Holy Spirit did the rest. God transformed Josefina and her struggle with anger vanished. Christ helped her to speak gently to her kids and respect their father. She was soon baptized. Just fifteen days after her conversion, Josefina opened her home to host a new cell, which has now multiplied four times.

Elim has been penetrating the entire city of San Salvador with the gospel, primary through friendship evangelism and mother-daughter cell multiplication.[30]

---

30. If a targeted area cannot easily be reached by multiplying a group, Elim is finding that it is often better to look for someone in that area to open

INTERNATIONAL CHARISMATIC MISSION, BOGOTA, COLOMBIA

Today, most people associate Colombia with guerilla warfare, drug addicts, and spiritual darkness. They don't know that in the midst of the darkness, God is building his church. One missionary to Colombia said, "Without the security issues, there would not be the urgency of the task."[31] The International Charismatic Mission is not the only church growing in Colombia, but it is a leading cell church that in 1996 had grown to approximately 10,000 cells. César Castellanos commented, "We've grown so much that we don't even count people anymore—just cell groups."[32]

Late in 1982, César Castellanos, a disillusioned young pastor in Colombia, quit his pastoral ministry. He was no longer satisfied in the pastorate and decided that it was better to resign. Four months later, however, God gave hiim a vision that changed the direction of his life. Recounting that experience, Castellanos said that God told him,

> Dream of a very large church, because dreams are the language of my Spirit. Because the people in the church that you will pastor will be as numerous as the

---

their home for a cell plant and then provide a trained leader to start a new group.

31. Steve Irvin, a personal friend, made this statement to me. He was a missionary in Colombia for over twenty years. Steve, in fact, fueled my small group vision by giving me a small group manual in 1991 in Quito, Ecuador.

32. César Castellanos, *Sueña y Ganarás el Mundo*, 87.

> stars of heaven and as the sands of the sea, the multitude will not be able to be counted."[33]

In response to that vision in February of 1983, International Charismatic Mission (ICM) was birthed in Bogota, Colombia. Although Castellanos had never before pastored a church of over 120 people, he knew from the vision that God gave him that now he was to lead a church with an innumerable multitude of people.

TRIP TO KOREA

Pastor César's trip to Korea in 1986 provided foundational principles for establishing a cell church system. He and his wife Claudia returned transformed by the potential for multiplying cell groups. Castellanos always believed in the role of small groups, but in 1986, he grasped the need for a cell church system as the way to support the growth of small groups.

Having only one model to follow, ICM copied Cho's system in its entirety. Pastor César organized his small groups geographically throughout Bogota. As he reflected back, he acknowledged that the early system needed fine-tuning. While copying the entire model, he failed to adapt it to his own cultural context. ICM limped along from 1986 to 1991, sensing that something was missing. The church grew to about seventy cells, but they felt God wanted more for them.

---

33. Joel Comiskey, *Home Cell Group Explosion: How Your Small Group Can Grow and Multiply* (Houston, TX: Touch Publications, 1998).

EVERYONE PREPARED TO MINISTER

Castellanos became frustrated with the Cho cell methodology because it took too long to produce cell leaders—a full two years. Castellanos noticed that few of the people who began the equipping process actually completed the training and those that did had lost their non-Christian friends due to the long time it took to complete the course. Castellanos felt that God gave him a breakthrough. He said to God, "Lord, I need something that would help me accelerate the purpose." He felt God saying to him, "I'm going to give you the ability to train people quickly."[34]

Castellanos credits Jesus's example of discipling twelve people as the biblical inspiration for this method. Some of the insights that Castellanos implemented were:

1. A "consolidation" process to disciple new believers that almost immediately sends them on a weekend "Encounter" retreat to help them be set free from spiritual bondage and be filled with the Holy Spirit. This discipleship system then equips every cell member to start their own cell group within the first year of coming to Christ while remaining in their parent cell.
2. An emphasis on the multiplication of homogeneous cell groups targeting specific populations such as men, women, youth, professionals, and children.
3. A system of oversight that has cell leaders in "groups of twelve" where they meet and are discipled on a weekly

34. For more information, read, Joel Comiskey *Groups of Twelve: A New Way to Mobilize Leaders and Multiply Groups in Your Church* (Moreno Valley, CA: CCS Publishing, 1999).

> basis. Leaders of the groups of twelve are also members in another group of twelve led by someone else.

The G-12 methodology is now being implemented with many variations in cell churches in various parts of the world. The diffusion of the G-12 method has been promoted by the large annual conferences that the ICM Church holds and by international conferences that Castellanos has been leading in the United States and Europe.[35]

KEY G-12 PRINCIPLES

Although there are many principles that ICM emphasizes, it seems that three stand out above the others. They are:

Principle #1: Everyone who enters the church is a potential cell leader. The declared goal of ICM is to transform every new convert into a dynamic cell leader.[36] Pastor Castellanos counsels his cell leaders to envision each member of the cell as a future cell leader. No matter how set aside or broken down because of sin, Castellanos believes that God is all powerful and able to make something beautiful of each person.

Some pastors and leaders believe that only those with the gift of evangelism or the gift of leadership are capable of leading a cell group. The goal is to discover "the gifted" in the congregation and then to train them to lead cell groups. One pastor,

---

35. Jim Egli, "What Do I Do with the G-12 Model? Insights from Those Who Have Begun the Journey," *CellChurch* (Volume 7, Number 4, Fall, 1998), p. 26.

36. This one point is repeated over and over again from the top leadership at ICM—not just César Castellanos.

emboldened by what God was doing at ICM said, "We do not speak of 'cell members' any longer, but of trainees to become cell leaders."[37]

Core Principle #2: All believers are expected to enter the cell leader equipping process. ICM asks everyone to enter the equipping process to eventually become a cell leader (the training track includes a three-day retreat and classroom training). As soon as a new convert starts attending ICM, he or she is placed on the training path that ends in cell leadership. Involvement at ICM means entering the equipping track.

Core Principle #3: Every leader is a potential supervisor. The G-12 model asks each parent cell leader to supervise those new leaders who come from the parent cell. Supervisors are not appointed in the G-12 model. No one is waiting for a "calling" from above to become a supervisor.[38]

The G-12 system taps into the personal motivation of each individual leader. All energetic, entrepreneurial leaders can rise as high as their drive takes them. They can supervise (disciple) as many new leaders as their time and talents permit.

---

37. Harold F. Weitsz, *Quest for the Perfect Pastoral System* (Little Falls Christian Centre, Little Falls, Roodepoort, South Africa), p. 4.

38. In the original cell model founded by David Cho, when five cells were formed, a supervisor was appointed to rotate among those five cells. The appointed supervisor was asked to stop leading his cell group in order to care for five groups. When five supervisors emerged (each over five cells), a zone pastor was appointed to care for those supervisors. This process of appointment continued upward to the office of district pastor who cared for the zone pastors. No one rose higher unless he or she received an invitation to assume the position.

G-12 EXCESSES AND CONCERNS

While ICM added innovation to the cell church movement worldwide, it began to promote the superiority of its own model, asking churches to adopt the ICM model in its entirety, rather than adapting the cell strategy to each context—like they themselves adapted Cho's model to fit their own context. I've included some of those excesses and concerns on my website.[39]

CELL-BASED MOVEMENT IN BRAZIL

Brazil is a unique country. It boasts the largest tropical rain forest in the world, enormous desert regions, and countless beaches. There are also a wide variety of traditions and cultural patterns. Brazil is also a land where the Spirit of God is moving in a unique way. And part of God's special *kingdom work* in Brazil is the rapid growth of cell churches. Neville Chamberlin writes, "Whole denominations, like the Baptists and Assemblies of God, are deciding to transition their churches—hundreds of them—to cells . . ."[40]

IGREJA DA PAZ

Luke Huber, a North American missionary kid born and raised in Brazil, started the Paz Church in 1976 when he came to Santarem, a city in Northern Brazil. Luke died in a plane accident in 1994 while ministering to the tribal people in northern

---

39. In 2002 I wrote about the excesses of the G-12 movement, which have only worsened over time. You can find these comments here: http://www.joelcomiskeygroup.com/articles/coaching/concernsG12.htm

40. Neville Chamberlin, Cell Church Missions Network, News Roundup #54. Received 6/16/2000.

Brazil. His younger brother, Abe Huber, took charge of the Paz Church and transitioned the Paz churches to become cell churches and started spreading the cell-church-planting vision.[41]

The goal is for each person in the church to plant an evangelistic cell group (Igreja da Paz defines their cell groups in the same way that Elim defines a cell group), multiply it, and to even plant an Igreja da Paz Church. This "effort" has resulted in planting hundreds of churches throughout Brazil.

One innovation of Igreja da Paz is its emphasis on both large and small churches. Huber realizes that it takes all kinds to get the job done. In 2014, the mother church in Santarem had 60,000 people in over 7,000 cell groups and 400 Paz churches in the region. The churches are linked together in a similar cell church vision. Some of the Igreja da Paz churches are very small and only a few minutes from the large mother church.

Most of these local churches follow the same strategy, but it's not a requirement. Each church is self-governing, have their own place to meet, and maintain a fraternal relationship with the Igreja da Paz movement. In 2006, Igreja da Paz started another church-planting movement in the Northwestern part of Brazil. This new endeavor has grown to approximately eighty churches with the mother church in Fortaleza numbering

---

41. Igreja da Paz; Location: Santarem and Fortaleza, Brazil; Senior Pastor: Abe Huber; Background: Non-denominational Igreja da Paz was started in 1980 and in 2014 had 14,000 cell groups and 90,000 people in their network of churches. Web site: igrejadapaz.com.br. I stayed at Abe's home in 2002 while doing a conference at his church. I found Abe to act more Brazilian in culture than North American. After each evening service, for example, he preferred to hang out with fellow Brazilians into the wee hours of the morning. "That's just Abe," his coworkers told me. He married a Brazilian.

some seven thousand five hundred people and one thousand three cells.

Igreja da Paz emphasizes one-on-one discipleship. Abe was personally impacted as a youth through the one-on-one discipleship method, and he hasn't forgotten those early lessons. He's integrated one-on-one discipleship into the church's training process. Each person that comes to a celebration service or a cell group is assigned a one-on-one mentor. The entire process is called MDA—Micro Discipleship Strategy.

Huber is a gifted apostle, able to lead his huge mother church, but he realizes that many leaders don't have those same gifts. They will do better at pastoring much smaller churches, and the Paz Church does an excellent job of preparing an army of church planters through cell ministry.

ROBERT LAY AND SLOW, STEADY GROWTH

Many have read the old English story of the hare (rabbit) and the tortoise (turtle), which is one of Aesop's Fables. In the story, the rabbit ridiculed the turtle for having short feet and a slow pace. The turtle replied, "Though you be swift as the wind, I will beat you in a race." The rabbit agreed to a race, believing that the turtle could never win. The two started the race together, and the turtle never stopped, following a slow but steady pace to the end of the course. The rabbit, lying down by the wayside, fell fast asleep. At last waking up, and moving as fast as he could, he realized the turtle had already finished and won the race.

This story has played out in the cell church in Brazil. Some cell models, like the rabbit, entered Brazil and offered quick growth and the promise of rapid numbers. Many churches followed these models in search of painless, miraculous, and rapid growth. For example, the G-12 model entered Brazil like a storm in early 2000. Many jumped on board the G-12 movement, only to later leave discouraged and disillusioned. Seeking rapid growth, these pastors abandoned the slow, steady growth based on cell principles, like those principles embraced by Robert Lay and *Ministerio Igreja em Células* (Ministry of Cell-Based Churches).

No ministry has had a greater impact of resourcing the Brazilian church than Robert Lay's ministry. Pastor Robert Lay came into contact with the cell church vision back in the early 1980s, while obtaining a Master's degree in the United States. God lit a passion in his life to make disciples through New Testament house-to-house ministry. He returned to Brazil and successfully introduced these cell concepts in his home church, Mennonite Brethren Church of Curitiba (State of Paraná, Brazil).

After establishing cell ministry in his own church, God called Robert to spread this vision to bless other churches in Brazil. He became the official TOUCH representative in Brazil.[42] His organization began teaching four different cell church modules in the Portuguese language. These modules (adapted from Neighbour's *Year of the Transition*) taught churches how to make the cell church transition. Lay's ministry also translated and published cell church literature in Portuguese.

Since its inception in 1997, the purpose of Ministerio Igreja em Células was always to teach values, principles, and to network pastors and leaders together on the cell church journey.

---

42. TOUCH is a cell resource ministry first established by Ralph Neighbour in the 1990s in Houston, Texas.

Some criticized Robert Lay's ministry as being too "turtle-like." They felt that he and his ministry over-emphasized cell church theology, values, starting with a prototype, and making transitional change in a slow, steady manner.

So what are the results? Since the initial training in 1998, *Ministerio Igreja em Células* has trained over sixteen thousand pastors and leaders in cell church principles and values. After many years of consistently teaching the values and principles, there are now large, healthy cell churches from many, many denominations in Brazil. In addition to teaching the modules, Lay's ministry has added two national conferences, five regional conferences per year, and translated over seventy cell church books into Portuguese.

Many of the largest, healthiest cell churches in Brazil have gone through the transitioning process and now have hundreds of cell groups. The resource ministry of *Ministerio Igreja em Células* has helped churches to avoid the pitfalls during the transition.

The good news is that many churches who took the time to study cell church principles and network with other pastors are now shining models for others to follow. On the other hand, many of the "quick growth" churches are realizing that the glitter quickly fades in the reality of day-to-day cell church ministry. Some are now rejoining Robert Lay's network. Turtle-like ministry requires long-term persistence, passion, and perseverance. It's easy to give up along the way, or jump on the bandwagon of the latest, greatest success story in an attempt to achieve rapid growth.

There are still many obstacles and struggles, since Brazilians tend to want things to happen instantaneously. Many churches cut corners and don't take the time to build a strong foundation of values. Yet, many more, having persevered, are shining example of God's work in cell-based churches.

WORLDWIDE EMPHASIS ON SMALLER, REPRODUCIBLE CELL CHURCHES

In the cell church movement worldwide, there is a renewed interest in planting smaller, more reproducible cell churches. The fact is that the vast majority of pastors around the world are not called to manage a large celebration gathering. God has simply not gifted them to do so. Administrating such a large church involves managing details that most people are simply not equipped to handle.

Paul the apostle was the most effective missionary church planter of the first century. He planted simple, reproducible churches and moved on to spread the gospel. He could say "So from Jerusalem all the way around to Illyricum, I have fully proclaimed the gospel of Christ" (Romans 15:19). Before AD 47 there were no churches in these provinces. In AD 57 Paul spoke of his work being accomplished.

Ben Wong, founder of Grace Church, has dedicated his life to plant reproducible cell churches around the world. Ben wasn't content with simply growing his own church. He realized that Great Commission ministry can only be accomplished through simple, reproducible cell church planting. Ben writes,

> Small churches comprise the great majority of churches in the world. Most pastors became pastors because they love God and desire to love his people. The reality is that in a small church, this can happen most effectively. In fact to become larger than 80 people, the pastor will need to become more administrative, and he may need

> a skill he does not have. Large churches need entrepreneurs, and very few pastors are like this.[43]

Jimmy Seibert, the founding pastor of Antioch Community Church in Waco, Texas, was radically transformed at the age of seventeen. He started small groups on the Baylor University campus that eventually grew to six hundred students on four campuses. He and some of the students wrote a book called *Reaching College Students through Cells.* In 1999 Jimmy started ACC.

ACC has never been content to grow one church larger and larger. Yet as the mother church gives itself away, it has continued to grow over the years. Like the New Testament church, God has called them to become a church planting movement. As of 2010, ACC has sent forty church planting teams all over the world (to twenty-four nations). They also have a missionary support staff numbering 450 from their own church.

Seibert believes that churches need to offer their people a practical missionary vision to reach the world. As a college pastor, he noticed that parachurch organizations were often more mission focused than the church. "God's plan is for the church to offer a world vision. Young people long to give themselves to a world-changing vision," Jimmy said.

ACC breathes the principle of multiplication—in their groups, leaders, churches, and missionaries. Each year ACC offers either a missions conference or a church planting conference on a rotating basis. Antioch believes and teaches the need for

---

43. Joel Comiskey, Sam Scaggs, Ben Wong, *You Can Coach* (Moreno Valley: CA: CCS Publishing, 2010), pp. 70-71.

brokenness and the filling of the Holy Spirit which result in radical obedience.

Bob Roberts, Jr., senior pastor of Northwood Church in Texas, has planted over one hundred churches. In his book, *The Multiplying Church*, he writes:

> On more than one occasion, I've found myself in a group of mega-church pastors who make a statement like this: "We need to partner to start some significant churches—we don't need to waste our time on these little churches of a hundred or two hundred." They don't get it! I try to educate them, but, more often than not, to no avail. When they make a statement like that, they miss two things. First, they don't know their history. Where faith has exploded, it has never been because of the multiplication of mega-churches, but of smaller churches from 50 to 200 . . . Second, they don't understand the nature of movements. Movements are personal and viral. Where movements have emerged, it hasn't been because of the large, but because of the small.[44]

When Jesus saw the incredible needs around him and especially those who were helpless and harassed and in need of a shepherd, he said to his disciples, "The harvest is plentiful but the workers are few. Ask the Lord of the harvest, therefore, to send out workers into his harvest field" (Matthew 9:37-38).

As I travel around the world, I passionately plead with larger cell churches to hear God's call for missions. I would love to

---

44. Bob Roberts, Jr., *The Multiplying Church: The New Math for Starting New Churches* (Grand Rapids, MI: Zondervan, 2008), p. 65.

see leaders who have multiplied cells and now supervise cells to consider becoming missionary church planters all over the world. Senior pastors are the key to releasing such people. Some of these multiplication pastors will plant nearby in the same city, state, or country. Others will become cross-cultural missionaries to plant cell churches on distant shores. The best church planters are those who have multiplied cell groups and supervised the new leaders. They possess the vital, needed experience to plant a church.

LESSONS LEARNED

- The worldwide cell church movement stands on the shoulders of prior small group foundations. Each small group movement in history has offered key principles and glimpses of a better way to minister.
- Cell churches draw their strength from New Testament Christianity and discover their motivation and inward drive from New Testament principles.
- Beyond the bedrock biblical base for cell ministry, cell churches draw on common principles: holistic definition of a cell, cells as the base of the church, leadership vision coming from lead pastor and leadership team, and the power of prayer.
- There is a danger of following one model and then concluding that it's the only true model.
- The modern day cell church movement is leaning more and more toward simple, reproducible cell church planting, rather than emphasizing growing one church to an enormous size. Both larger cell churches and smaller, more reproducible cell churches will always exist side-by-side.

Conclusion

WHERE DO WE GO FROM HERE?

The cell church phenomenon is here to stay. New creative models are surfacing as the cell church adapts to different environments and cultures. Ralph Neighbour, Jr., opens his 1990 book *Where Do We Go From Here?* with the declaration: "I am convinced that the traditional church worldwide is being slowly replaced by an act of God. Developments taking place today are as powerful as the upheaval in 1517 during the time of Martin Luther."[1] Concurring with Neighbour in a 1993 article in *CellChurch* magazine, church growth strategist Carl George proclaimed,

1. Neighbour Jr., p. 6.

> In fact, what the Holy Spirit wants to do may be even more radical than what Dr. Neighbour is prophesying! In Christian communities from Orthodox to Anabaptist, Pentecostal to Lutheran, the notion of a cell-driven church is completely reorienting our understanding of the nature of ministry.[2]

Do we stand at the onset of a second reformation? What is God doing in the church and the world today? What church transformation can we expect to see in the twenty-first century in North America and around the world?

Although the cell movement has yet to capture the attention of the broader church, it does indeed appear that we may stand at the onset of something big. What began in an out-of-the-way church in Seoul, South Korea, has now swept into every continent.

Interest in the cell methodology has been up and down over the last couple of decades, but the movement continues to experience tremendous growth. Though the diffusion of the cell strategy has mushroomed in some countries such as Latin America, South Africa, Brazil, Singapore, Korea, and Russia, in many locations it will take much longer before the innovation gains wide acceptance.

In his outstanding book, *Diffusion of Innovations,* communication scholar, Everett Rogers, points out that diffusion studies have consistently demonstrated an S-Curve pattern.[3] A successful

---

2. Carl George, "What Is a Meta-Church? (And How Does it Differ from a Cell Church?)" *CellChurch* (Volume 2, Issue 2, 1993), p. 5.

3. Everett Rogers, *Diffusion of Innovations,* Fourth Edition. (New York: Free Press, 1995), p. 322.

innovation always begins slowly, but it reaches a point of critical mass when diffusion rapidly accelerates. Sometimes the span of time between the beginning of the innovation and its rapid diffusion is years, at times it is decades and sometimes it is even centuries. The twentieth century cell movement began thirty-five years ago in 1964. It is growing significantly now, but I predict that it will likely not reach a point of critical mass in most countries for years to come.

One of the most significant realities pointing to the need for the cell-based church is the times in which we live. Sociologists and historians have pointed out that the twenty-first century world will look much like that of the first century. It will be a time of rapid urbanization, of moral decay, and increasing religious pluralism. Many Christians and churches are frightened by this scenario. Yet this is just the type of environment that the early church thrived in, as it spread from house-to-house across the Roman Empire.

God is transforming the church in the midst of a tremendous upheaval, but it is important for those in the cell movement to realize that the cell methodology is only one part of this divine upheaval. We must take heed to the words that echo throughout the opening chapters of the book of Revelation, "He who has an ear, let him hear what the Spirit says to the churches."

RESOURCES BY JOEL COMISKEY

You can find all of Joel Comiskey's books at *Joel Comiskey Group*

Phone: 1-888-511-9995

Website: www.joelcomiskeygroup.com

Joel Comiskey's previous books cover the following topics

- Leading a cell group (*How to Lead a Great Cell Group Meeting*, 2001, 2009).
- How to multiply the cell group (*Home Cell Group Explosion*, 1998).
- How to prepare spiritually for cell ministry (*An Appointment with the King*, 2002, 2011).
- How to practically organize your cell system (*Reap the Harvest*, 1999; *Cell Church Explosion*, 2004).
- How to train future cell leaders (*Leadership Explosion*, 2001; *Live*, 2007; *Encounter*, 2007; *Grow*, 2007; *Share*, 2007; *Lead*, 2007; *Coach*, 2008; *Discover*, 2008).
- How to coach/care for cell leaders (*How to be a Great Cell Group Coach*, 2003; *Groups of Twelve*, 2000; *From Twelve to Three*, 2002).
- How the gifts of the Spirit work within the cell group (*The Spirit-filled Small Group*, 2005, 2009; *Discover*, 2008).
- How to fine tune your cell system (*Making Cell Groups Work Navigation Guide*, 2003).
- Principles from the second largest church in the world (*Passion and Persistence*, 2004).
- How cell church works in North America (*The Church that Multiplies*, 2007, 2009).
- How to plant a church (*Planting Churches that Reproduce*, 2009)
- How to be a relational disciple (*Relational Disciple*, 2010).
- How to distinguish truth from myths (*Myths and Truths of the Cell Church*, 2011).
- What the Biblical foundations for cell church are (*Biblical Foundations for the Cell-Based Church*, 2012, *Making Disciples in the Cell-Based Church*, 2013).

How To Lead A Great Cell Group Meeting: *So People Want to Come Back*

Do people expectantly return to your group meetings every week? Do you have fun and experience joy during your meetings? Is everyone participating in discussion and ministry? You can lead a great cell group meeting, one that is life changing and dynamic. Most people don't realize that they can create a God-filled atmosphere because they don't know how. Now the secret is out. This guide will show you how to:

- Prepare yourself spiritually to hear God during the meeting
- Structure the meeting so it flows
- Spur people in the group to participate and share their lives openly
- Share your life with others in the group
- Create stimulating questions
- Listen effectively to discover what is transpiring in others' lives
- Encourage and edify group members
- Open the group to non-Christians
- See the details that create a warm atmosphere

By implementing these time-tested ideas, your group meetings will become the hot-item of your members' week. They will go home wanting more and return each week bringing new people with them. 140 pgs.

Home Cell Group Explosion: *How Your Small Group Can Grow and Multiply*

The book crystallizes the author's findings in some eighteen areas of research, based on a meticulous questionnaire that he submitted to cell church leaders in eight countries around the world, locations that he also visited personally for his research. The detailed notes in the back of the book offer the student of cell church growth a rich mine for further reading. The beauty of Comiskey's book is that he not only summarizes his survey results in a thoroughly convincing way but goes on to analyze in practical ways many of his survey results in separate chapters. The happy result is that any cell church leader, intern or member completing this quick read will have his priorities/values clearly aligned and ready to be followed-up. If you are a pastor or small group leader, you should devour this book! It will encourage you and give you simple, practical steps for dynamic small group life and growth. 175 pgs.

An Appointment with the King: *Ideas for Jump-Starting Your Devotional Life*

With full calendars and long lists of things to do, people often put on hold life's most important goal: building an intimate relationship with God. Often, believers wish to pursue the goal but are not sure how to do it. They feel frustrated or guilty when their attempts at personal devotions seem empty and unfruitful. With warm, encouraging writing, Joel Comiskey guides readers on how to set a daily appointment with the King and make it an exciting time they will look forward to. This book first answers the question "Where do I start?" with step-by-step instructions on how to spend time with God and practical ideas for experiencing him more fully. Second, it highlights the benefits of spending time with God, including joy, victory over sin, and spiritual guidance. The book will help Christians tap into God's resources on a daily basis, so that even in the midst of busyness they can walk with him in intimacy and abundance. 175 pgs.

Reap the Harvest: *How a Small Group SysSystem Can Grow System Can Grow Your Church*

Have you tried small groups and hit a brick wall? Have you wondered why your groups are not producing the fruit that was promised? Are you looking to make your small groups more effective? Cell-church specialist and pastor Dr. Joel Comiskey studied the world's most successful cell churches to determine why they grow. The key: They have embraced specific principles. Conversely, churches that do not embrace these same principles have problems with their groups and therefore do not grow. Cell churches are successful not because they have small groups but because they can support the groups. In this book, you will discover how these systems work. 236 pgs.

La Explosión de la Iglesia Celular: *Cómo Estructurar la Iglesia en Células Eficaces* (Editorial Clie, 2004)

This book is available only in Spanish and contains Joel Comiskey's research of eight of the world's largest cell churches, five of which reside in Latin America. It details how to make the transition from a traditional church to the cell church structure and many other valuable insights, including: the history of the cell church, how to organize your church to become a praying church, the most important principles of the cell church, and how to raise up an army of cell leaders. 236 pgs.

***Leadership Explosion:** Multiplying Cell Group Leaders to Reap the Harvest*

Some have said that cell groups are leader breeders. Yet even the best cell groups often have a leadership shortage. This shortage impedes growth and much of the harvest goes untouched. Joel Comiskey has discovered why some churches are better at raising up new cell leaders than others. These churches do more than pray and hope for new leaders. They have an intentional strategy, a plan that will quickly equip as many new leaders as possible. In this book, you will discover the training models these churches use to multiply leaders. You will discover the underlying principles of these models so that you can apply them. 202 pgs.

FIVE-BOOK EQUIPPING SERIES

#1: Live

#2: Encounter

#3: Grow

#4: Share

#5: Lead

The five book equipping series is designed to train a new believer all the way to leading his or her own cell group. Each of the five books contains eight lessons. Each lesson has interactive activities that helps the trainee reflect on the lesson in a personal, practical way.

Live starts the training by covering key Christian doctrines, including baptism and the Lord's supper. 85 pgs.
Encounter guides the believer to receive freedom from sinful bondages. The Encounter book can be used one-on-one or in a group. 91 pgs.
Grow gives step-by-step instruction for having a daily quiet time, so that the believer will be able to feed him or herself through spending daily time with God. 87 pgs.
Share instructs the believer how to communicate the gospel message in a winsome, personal way. This book also has two chapters on small group evangelism. 91 pgs.
Lead prepares the Christian on how to facilitate an effective cell group. This book would be great for those who form part of a small group team. 91 pgs.

TWO-BOOK ADVANCED TRAINING SERIES

Coach

Discover

Coach and ***Discover*** make-up the Advanced Training, prepared specifically to take a believer to the next level of maturity in Christ.

Coach prepares a believer to coach another cell leader. Those experienced in cell ministry often lack understanding on how to coach someone else. This book provides step-by-step instruction on how to coach a new cell leader from the first meeting all the way to giving birth to a new group. The book is divided into eight lessons, which are interactive and help the potential coach deal with real-life, practical coaching issues. 85 pgs.

Discover clarifies the twenty gifts of the Spirit mentioned in the New Testament. The second part shows the believer how to find and use his or her particular gift. This book is excellent to equip cell leaders to discover the giftedness of each member in the group. 91 pgs.

How to be a Great Cell Group Coach: *Practical insight for Supporting and Mentoring Cell Group Leaders*

Research has proven that the greatest contributor to cell group success is the quality of coaching provided for cell group leaders. Many are serving in the position of a coach, but they don't fully understand what they are supposed to do in this position. Joel Comiskey has identified seven habits of great cell group coaches. These include: Receiving from God, Listening to the needs of the cell group leader, Encouraging the cell group leader, Caring for the multiple aspects of a leader's life, Developing the cell leader in various aspects of leadership, Strategizing with the cell leader to create a plan, Challenging the cell leader to grow.

Practical insights on how to develop these seven habits are outlined in section one. Section two addresses how to polish your skills as a coach with instructions on diagnosing problems in a cell group, how to lead coaching meetings, and what to do when visiting a cell group meeting. This book will prepare you to be a great cell group coach, one who mentors, supports, and guides cell group leaders into great ministry. 139 pgs.

Groups of Twelve: *A New Way to Mobilize Leaders and Multiply Groups in Your Church*

This book clears the confusion about the Groups of 12 model. Joel dug deeply into the International Charismatic Mission in Bogota, Colombia and other G12 churches to learn the simple principles that G12 has to offer your church. This book also contrasts the G12 model with the classic 5x5 and shows you what to do with this new model of ministry. Through onsite research, international case studies, and practical experience, Joel Comiskey outlines the G12 principles that your church can use today.

Billy Hornsby, director of the Association of Related Churches, says, "Joel Comiskey shares insights as a leader who has himself raised up numerous leaders. From how to recognize potential leaders to cell leader training to time-tested principles of leadership—this book has it all. The accurate comparisons of various training models make it a great resource for those who desire more leaders. Great book!" 182 pgs.

From Twelve To Three: *How to Apply G12 Principles in Your Church*

The concept of the Groups of 12 began in Bogota, Colombia, but now it is sweeping the globe. Joel Comiskey has spent years researching the G12 structure and the principles behind it.

From his experience as a pastor, trainer, and consultant, he has discovered that there are two ways to embrace the G12 concept: adopting the entire model or applying the principles that support the model.

This book focuses on the application of principles rather than adoption of the entire model. It outlines the principles and provides a modified application which Joel calls the G12.3. This approach presents a pattern that is adaptable to many different church contexts.

The concluding section illustrates how to implement the G12.3 in various kinds of churches, including church plants, small churches, large churches, and churches that already have cells. 178 pgs.

The Spirit-filled Small Group: *Leading Your Group to Experience the Spiritual Gifts.*

The focus in many of today's small groups has shifted from Spirit-led transformation to just another teacher-student Bible study. But exercising every member's spiritual gifts is vital to the effectiveness of the group. With insight born of experience in more than twenty years of small group ministry, Joel Comiskey explains how leaders and participants alike can be supernaturally equipped to deal with real-life issues. Put these principles into practice and your small group will never be the same!
This book works well with Comiskey's training book, ***Discover.*** It fleshes out many of the principles in Comiskey's training book. Chuck Crismier, radio host, *Viewpoint,* writes, "Joel Comiskey has again provided the Body of Christ with an important tool to see God's Kingdom revealed in and through small groups." 191 pgs.

Making Cell Groups Work Navigation Guide: *A Toolbox of Ideas and Strategies for Transforming Your Church.*

For the first time, experts in cell group ministry have come together to provide you with a 600 page reference tool like no other. When Ralph Neighbour, Bill Beckham, Joel Comiskey and Randall Neighbour compiled new articles and information under careful orchestration and in-depth understanding that Scott Boren brings to the table, it's as powerful as private consulting! Joel Comiskey has an entire book within this mammoth 600 page work. There are also four additional authors.

Passion and Persistence: *How the Elim Church's Cell Groups Penetrated an Entire City for Jesus*

This book describes how the Elim Church in San Salvador grew from a small group to 116,000 people in 10,000 cell groups. Comiskey takes the principles from Elim and applies them to churches in North America and all over the world. Ralph Neighbour says: "I believe this book will be remember as one of the most important ever written about a cell church movement! I experienced the passion when visiting Elim many years ago. Comiskey's report about Elim is not a pattern to be slavishly copied. It is a journey into grasping the true theology and methodology of the New Testament church. You'll discover how the Elim Church fans into flame their passion for Jesus and His Word, how they organize their cells to penetrate a city and world for Jesus, and how they persist until God brings the fruit." 158 pgs.

The Church that Multiplies: *Growing a Healthy Cell Church in North America*

Does the cell church strategy work in North America? We hear about exciting cell churches in Colombia and Korea, but where are the dynamic North American cell churches? This book not only declares that the cell church concept does work in North America but dedicates an entire chapter to examining North American churches that are successfully using the cell strategy to grow in quality and quantity. This book provides the latest statistical research about the North American church and explains why the cell church approach restores health and growth to the church today. More than anything else, this book will provide practical solutions for pastors and lay leaders to use in implementing cell-based ministry. 181 pgs.

Planting Churches that Reproduce: *Planting a Network of Simple Churches*

What is the best way to plant churches in the 21st century? Comiskey believes that simple, reproducible church planting is most effective. The key is to plant churches that are simple enough to grow into a movement of churches. Comiskey has been gathering material for this book for the past fifteen Years. He has also planted three churches in a wide variety of settings. Planting Churches that Reproduce is the fruit of his research and personal experience. Comiskey uses the latest North American church planting statistics, but extends the illustrations to include worldwide church planting. More than anything else, this book will provide practical solutions for those planting churches today. Comiskey's book is a must-read book for all those interested in establishing Christ-honoring, multiplying churches. 176 pgs.

The Relational Disciple: *How God Uses Community to Shape Followers of Jesus*

Jesus lived with His disciples for three years and taught them life lessons as a group. After three years, he commanded them to "go and do likewise" (Matthew 28:18-20). Jesus discipled His followers through relationships—and He wants us to do the same. Scripture is full of exhortations to love and serve one another. This book will show you how. The isolation present in the western world is creating a hunger for community and the world is longing to see relational disciples in action. This book will encourage Christ-followers to allow God to use the natural relationships in life—family, friends, work relationships, cells, church, and missions to mold them into relational disciples.

You Can Coach: *How to Help Leaders Build Healthy Churches through Coaching*

We've entitled this book "You Can Coach" because we believe that coaching is more about passing on what you've lived and holding others accountable in the process. Coaching doesn't require a higher degree, special talent, unique personality, or a particular spiritual gift. We believe, in fact, that God wants coaching to become a movement. We long to see the day in which every pastor has a coach and in turn is coaching someone else. In this book, you'll hear three coaches who have successfully coached pastors for many years. They will share their history, dreams, principles, and what God is doing through coaching. Our hope is that you'll be both inspired and resourced to continue your own coaching ministry in the years to come.

Myths & Truths of the Cell Church: *Key Principles that Make or Break Cell Ministry*

Most of the modern day cell church movement is dynamic, positive, and applicable. As is true in most endeavors, errors and false assumptions have also cropped up to destroy an otherwise healthy movement. Sometimes these false concepts caused the church to go astray completely. At other times, they led the pastor and church down a dead-end road of fruitless ministry. Regardless of how the myths were generated, they had a chilling effect on the church's ministry. In this book, Joel Comiskey tackles these errors and false assumptions, helping pastors and leaders to untangle the webs of legalism that has crept into the cell church movement. Joel then guides the readers to apply biblical, time-tested principles that will guide them into fruitful cell ministry. Each chapter begins with a unique twist. Well-known worldwide cell church leaders open each chapter by answering questions to the chapter's topic in the form of an email dialogue. Whether you're starting out for the first time in cell ministry or a seasoned veteran, this book will give you the tools to help your ministry stay fresh and fruitful.

Biblical Foundations for the Cell-Based Church

Why cell church? Is it because David Cho's church is a cell church and happens to be the largest church in the history of Christianity? Is it because cell church is the strategy that many "great" churches are using?

Ralph Neighbour repeatedly says, "Theology must breed methodology."Joel Comiskey has arrived at the same conclusion. Biblical truth is the only firm foundation for anything we do. Without a biblical base, we don't have a strong under-pinning upon which we can hang our ministry and philosophy. We can plod through most anything when we know that God is stirring us to behave biblically.

Making Disciples in the Cell-Based Church

The primary goal of the church is to make disciples who make disciples. But how is the church supposed to do that? This book answers that question. Dr. Comiskey explains how both cell and celebration (larger gathering) work together in the process of making disciples. In the cell, a potential disciple is transformed through community, priesthood of all believers, group evangelism, and team multiplication. The cell system ensures each leader has a coach and that training happens. Then the cells gather together to worship and grow through the teaching of God's Word. This book will help you understand why and how to become a church that prioritizes discipleship.

What others are saying: I've read all of Joel Comiskey's books, but this one is his best work yet. I'm looking forward to having all of our pastors, coaches, cell leaders and members read this book in the near future. *Dr. Dennis Watson, Lead Pastor, Celebration Church of New Orleans*

I am so excited about Joel Comiskey□s new book, Making Disciples in the Twenty-First Century Church. Joel has unpacked discipleship, not just as an endeavor for individuals, but as the critical element for creating a church community and culture that reproduces the Kingdom of God all over the earth. *Jimmy Seibert, Senior Pastor, Antioch Community Church*

Like Joel□s other books, this one is solidly biblical, highly practical, wonderfully accessible and is grounded in Joel□s vast research and experience. *Dr. Dave Earley, Lead Pastor, Grace City Church of Las Vegas, Nevada*

INDEX

D

E

F

G

H

L

M

Q

R

U

V

W

Y

Z

Lightning Source UK Ltd.
Milton Keynes UK
UKOW04f2346140715

255174UK00002B/28/P